The Dialectics of Mania

Visions from a Mental Health Journey

By

Andrew Turtle

The Dialectics of Mania

Dedication

For all those who have experienced the dialectics of mania revelation or delusion.

Acknowledgment

The Dialectics of Mania was written during a time in which I was navigating a personal crisis. Although I gave many of you names that reflected how I perceived your roles and identities during the time we shared together, I would like to acknowledge all those who walked alongside me within Penrith Psychiatric Hospital, across both the Intensive Care and Acute Wards. This story could not have emerged without you.

Your strength gave me the courage to navigate the barriers I was facing within myself and within the system around me.

I would also like to acknowledge all those who experience the highs and lows of mental illness and who continue navigating the mental health system through both its good and difficult moments. In particular, I acknowledge those who experience the dialectics of mania — the tension between expansion and fragmentation, insight and illusion, awakening and disintegration.

You know the awakenings.

You know the fears.

You know the fragmentation and collapse that can emerge while walking alongside mania and all it has to throw at you.

May this work help bring language to experiences that are often difficult to explain.

Table of Contents

Before

One
DOOR
Mental Health

Prologue

There are seasons in life when everything appears steady, so steady that you begin to believe the storms of the past have finally quietened. For nearly twenty years, I lived in such a season. After a volatile adolescence marked by several psychotic episodes and three hospitalisations before the age of twenty, I carved out a long stretch of stability. I worked. I created. I took my place in the world with a steadiness that once felt unimaginable. Apart from subtle signs of *hypermania* beginning to creep in during the final year, I had been out of the hospital for almost two decades and had maintained full-time work for four and a half years.

The Dialectics of Mania begins at the moment that stability gave way.

At the time, I was employed by One Door Mental Health as an Engagement Officer, a peer support worker helping to establish a community-based mental health program. Alongside two colleagues, I helped build something deeply meaningful. It was a living expression of everything I believed in: peer support, lived experience leadership, and the possibility of transformation through shared humanity. We created a program that worked, one that people valued, relied on, and felt held by.

When the organisation restructured, reducing a team of twelve down to six, I was made redundant. The decision struck me with a strength I had not expected. It was not simply the loss of employment. It was the sudden collapse of something I had poured my heart, energy, and identity into. The grief of that loss opened a crack I did not yet recognise. On my final day, I contracted Covid-19. Illness weakened the body, grief weakened the centre, and together they set the stage for the unravelling that followed.

As my mental health declined, the hypermania intensified, and old patterns, once distant memories, returned with new force.

What emerged was a collision of the philosophical and esoteric frameworks that had shaped my worldview with the fragile state of a mind under strain. In the pages ahead, you will see this interplay clearly: mystical symbolism intertwining with delusional architecture, cosmological ideas sharpening into distorted revelations, and meaning appearing where structure had momentarily dissolved.

This blending was not accidental. For most of my life, I have searched for philosophical depth behind everyday experience, studying mysticism, metaphysics, cosmology, and the hidden architecture of consciousness. When my internal boundaries thinned, these inquiries surfaced raw and unfiltered. Mania amplified them, distorted them, and illuminated them all at once.

The Dialectics of Mania does not attempt to glorify or demonise that state. Instead, it explores its contradictions, its dialectics. Mania is both expansion and fragmentation, insight and illusion, awakening and disintegration. It exposes what is unhealed and magnifies what is sought. It brings both danger and revelation.

This book is a record of that threshold: the rupture, the meaning-making that surged through the chaos, and the slow reconstruction that followed. It chronicles a moment when constancy broke, when my search for meaning collided with psychological vulnerability, and when the esoteric and the delusional became indistinguishable long enough to show me something I could not have otherwise seen.

It begins when the ground gives way and continues into the long work of finding centre again.

Introduction

The Dialectics of Mania embarks on a journey that saw my mental state spiral into a steady decline over several months, eventually culminating in a hypomanic and psychotic episode that shattered the boundaries of my reality. During this tumultuous period, I became convinced I was reenacting the Biblical creation story here on Earth, an era I called "the last days." I believed I held the solutions to all the world's problems and was destined to usher in a 'New Dawn.' In an earnest attempt to share my vision and reshape the world, I was eventually confronted by police and transported to the Nepean Psychiatric Ward in an ambulance.

The narrative explores the events leading up to my hospitalisation and my subsequent experiences within the confines of the psychiatric ward. It culminates in my departure from the ward. As I grappled with the grips of mania, I traversed the shifting boundaries between dissociation and psychosis. Within this altered mental landscape, a series of extraordinary events unfolded. Wrestling with profound questions about creation and evolution, I envisioned the world's imminent end, a cosmic convergence of all the major sources of light in the universe. This represented a momentous juncture in the history of humanity and the universe, a convergence of the entire creation story that led to its conclusion.

I meticulously documented these defining moments as they occurred. As you journey through the pages of *The Dialectics of Mania*, you are left with the question of whether the occurrences and insights presented as my mental health declined are the stuff of myth, the byproduct of delusion, or revelatory insights into the universe's inner workings. That question, dear reader, I leave up to you.

The Gift Seeker

I met the Gift Seeker in a tranquil park. She wandered in search of her tribe, hoping to find respite from the heavy burden of depression and anxiety she had shouldered alone for years. Her General Practitioner had introduced her to One Door, a pivotal moment that would unlock countless doors in her life. That day, her support worker had driven her to the park, where she sat serenely, sipping her coffee, lost in thought.

The Gift Seeker was an extraordinary soul, kind, outgoing, honest, and loving. There was something undeniably special about her. We shared an instant connection, as she had grown dissatisfied with the support she had been receiving. She had a clear vision of what she needed, yet no one seemed to listen. Together, we embarked on a journey through the program we had tailored to her needs. One Door became the gateway that helped her step outside her home, meet new people, and explore horizons that had long been obscured, a passage to a brand-new world.

Our final day together at One Door was nothing short of electric. As always, fifteen or sixteen souls gathered within the centre, preparing a sumptuous feast. Laughter and camaraderie filled the air as we celebrated Daniel's birthday, singing in unison before presenting him with heartfelt cards and gifts. Overwhelmed with emotion, the Gift Seeker exclaimed, "This is my family!" At that moment, I realised my true gift: the Gift Seeker and the One Door Family had taught me the profound importance of finding one's tribe.

Descent

Beyond the Depths of Despair

I hit rock bottom when I lost my job at One Door, where I had poured my heart and soul into a unique mental health program. I had left behind a United Family and a position I had worked tirelessly to excel in. Seeking new opportunities, I ventured into a different area of employment, one where I considered myself an expert and the professionals around me validated that expertise. Together, we crafted an exceptional mental health program, largely inspired by my vision of an ideal mental health system. Yet, despite all our efforts, I felt defeated. My ongoing battle with mental health issues continued to obstruct my progress.

Leaving One Door also meant severing connections I had painstakingly nurtured. These relationships, built on trust and emotional investment, offered a safe space for individuals to open up about traumas that once trapped them in despair. I want to emphasise that I do not blame the Visionless leader; contractual obligations are important. However, there comes a time when making a difference should take precedence over metrics that lack true meaning. It should be about the quality of life, the people, and the meaningful connections we build. True healing happens when we walk together, supporting each other on the path to recovery.

My despair deepened. My Best Friend found me on the couch, dissociated in my thoughts. She reached out to her friend, who, as it turned out, was an Over-Promiser. In hindsight, I should have heeded my best friend's caution, but the offer seemed too enticing to resist. I eagerly jumped on the Consultancy bandwagon.

At first, things looked promising. The induction was impressive, and the team seemed thrilled to have me on board. I diligently crunched the numbers and studied the demographics. There was an air of optimism. Bipolar was under control now, but there was a noticeable void in leadership. I was told that I needed to "make a difference in their lives," meet the participants in their homes, and "make their dreams come true." It sounded too good to be true.

Weeks passed, and I began visiting people in their homes, filling out "expressions of interest," and crafting ways to fulfil their dreams. However, I inadvertently stepped on the toes of my colleagues, feeling increasingly stressed and out of my depth. I had constructed an impressive program on my own, with no help from Bipolar or The Over-Promiser. It all came to a head when Bipolar and The Over-Promiser sat me down and delivered the harsh truth: "Things are not working out."

Once again, another job slipped through my fingers. I felt defeated, crushed, and utterly disheartened. My heart sank, and my sense of self-worth plummeted. I had tried my hardest to fit in and laboured to make a positive impact, but success seemed to elude me. Once more, I felt utterly defeated, my spirit drained of all resolve.

Alone in the depths of despair, I contemplated the unfathomable. I lined concrete walls along my path, but lacked the strength to let go of my body and crash into the unyielding brick and mortar. I aligned my car's wheels with trees, accelerating to reckless speeds, yet I could not summon the courage to leave my bloodstain on the leaves and branches. For twelve agonising hours, I grappled with thoughts of ending my life. I decided to indulge in one last sumptuous meal, then retreat to one of my favourite places, drowning my sorrows until my liver ceased functioning. There, hidden from the world, I would remain undiscovered.

Returning home, I emptied my alcohol collection and concocted a story about visiting My Best Friend's house to do laundry. In my washing basket, I concealed bottles of alcohol, my final act of rebellion against a world that seemed to have given up on me. I sent My Best Friend a text detailing all the reasons why I felt I did not deserve to live. At first, she hung up on me, unable to tolerate my negative attitude. Yet, in her unwavering support, she ultimately listened. I stayed with her until I could no longer resist the pull of alcohol. Then, I yearned to be alone for my last hours on this planet. But when the moment came, I could not find the strength to endure it.

Goddess, She Does Not Care

Several months had passed, and I believed I had encountered my Goddess. At a time when I felt I had plummeted to the depths of despair, convinced that things could not possibly deteriorate further, I found myself checking into Ramsey Clinic, the very place where I had received care almost two decades ago. On my first day there, I encountered what I can only describe as an angel, a moment of absolute certainty. I was convinced that I had finally met the person I had been searching for, the one I believed to be my Goddess.

Initially, I viewed this woman as my ticket out of a troublesome relationship, not one with a challenging partner but with a woman deeply connected to an exceptionally difficult child. This child seemed unable to recognise the harm caused by their actions, readily justifying impulsive and dangerous behaviour. My previous four-and-a-half-year relationship had been profoundly loving, with my best friend as my closest companion.

As I referred to her, this Goddess appeared to be the escape I desperately needed. We quickly formed a connection, bonding over a shared interest in a topic that had long been suppressed in me, sexuality.

Upon leaving the hospital, my mind swirled with thoughts of her beauty. Though we had not yet consummated our relationship, we had explored various forms of physical intimacy that did not involve intercourse. Still, anxiety gripped me as I nervously drove to her house on the first day of my release. It was there, at last, that we discovered the depths of our passion. Our relationship was initially rooted in lust, but the intensity of our connection was undeniable. When I made love to her, it felt as though our bodies and souls melded into one, moving in perfect harmony. Every moment seemed imbued with profound purpose, as if our union had been destined. Her touch was delicate, her kiss pure, and when we made love, it felt like we were two halves becoming whole.

We entered a blissful honeymoon phase, with weeks flying by. I even introduced her to my parents during a visit to their home, where we spent a delightful weekend together. During our drive through Penrith, I first glimpsed her temper, but it was a minor blip in an otherwise enjoyable weekend. We also enjoyed spending time at a friend's bed and breakfast near my parents' house.

We revelled in countless romantic walks along the beach, hand in hand, and explored the beauty of her hometown, Newcastle. My birthday and Christmas came, and I was over the moon, except for a few fleeting moments when suicidal thoughts resurfaced. Despite a few bumps, I believed I had settled into my new life.

But on Christmas Eve, everything came crashing down. I had been working on a poem, preparing to make my mark on the world. I was ready to share this poem with everyone:

An electron freed from its cloud,
Powers the charge of the very first atom,
Of a body of particles, atoms, and chemicals,
Allowing information to flow through channels,
That expresses the mind,
A field of habit, emotion, and thought,
A life force that enables survival,
Provides a function to emerge,
And find balance as it adapts to change.
In the safety and security of desire,
I express my identity,
To fulfil and satisfy completeness,
Through the moral guidance of intention,
I search for context within reason,
So that I can discover the order
And bring the form to uncertainty.
I am complete,

Only as far as my potential gives me the capacity to fulfil my destiny.

Hindsight reveals that it was not a message meant to change the world, but in that manic and exhilarating moment, it felt beautiful. However, she swiftly silenced me.

She said, "Why would anyone bother reading what you write? What sets you apart from everyone else?" Or something to that effect. It was a painful blow. I had poured my heart and soul into sharing the insights I had gathered from a lifetime of research and discovery. I had honed the ability to express my ideas concisely, hoping to connect with others. But the Goddess did not take the time to read my writing; she dismissed it with a flick. No one was listening.

I erupted in frustration. All I craved for was to share the knowledge I had painstakingly attained and contribute to making the world a better place. I had dedicated my life to this mission, but no one cared. At that moment, I shut down completely.

Chaos

I woke up engulfed in misery on what should have been a sacred day. My mood was terrible, weighed down by the persistent feeling of being unheard and disregarded. The Goddess, my partner, incessantly voiced her longing for a single Christmas—just one—where her expectations took precedence. She yearned for a holiday season centred around her desires, yet she was not inclined to listen to my wishes. She remained closed off to my thoughts and even refused to read what I believed to be my message to the world. So, we mechanically carried on with our Christmas rituals, exchanging gifts and sharing breakfast. However, there was a conspicuous absence of joy and spirit. The festivities felt hollow and forced, prompting me to abandon my new home and retreat to my old one, overwhelmed by a sense of dejection.

As I journeyed back, Chaos seemed to descend upon me. It was as if my brain had reached its limits, with every neuron firing simultaneously. I wondered what it must have been like for God in the empty void before creation, before a single particle, atom, or human being had graced the universe. It was an expanse of emptiness, darkness, and desolation, devoid of awareness, touch, or connection. Driving my lonely little Holden Astra felt the same, an experience with no substance, as if I were operating a machine without purpose.

Then, a moment of enlightenment engulfed me. I felt as though I possessed all-encompassing knowledge, with every theory I had ever explored flashing across the screen of my mind. That knowledge vanished the next instant, leaving my mind utterly blank. Everything that had led up to that point flickered in and out like a blank canvas.

I contemplated suicide. I thought about driving my Holden Astra off Mooney Mooney Bridge. But the next moment, I reflected on how such an act would render my existence meaningless, leaving only an empty void. Everything I had worked for until then would be erased, useless, and pointless. Then joy surged within me, followed swiftly by anger. It was a whirlwind of emotions, each giving way to the next. Nothing seemed enduring, and nothing appeared to make sense for long. However, there were moments when everything clicked into place, offering profound meaning to all that had come before. But just as quickly, the next moment would return to a sense of meaninglessness.

It seemed as though our purpose on this planet was merely to exist. Yet if God were absent, what was the point of existence? What purpose did anything serve in a world devoid of meaning? There was nothing to strive for, work towards, or external motivation. It seemed as though our sole purpose was to exist. But then the act of existence felt magnificent, as it meant simply being in harmony with the planet, society, and the universe. Everything unfolded differently with every passing second. I seemed to inhale, then pause in nothingness, and then exhale. It was an experience that was simultaneously awe-inspiring, terrifying, frustrating, bizarre, and fascinating. Chaos and complete order coexisted in what felt like a single, fleeting moment.

As I reached the end of the freeway, a sense of calm and clarity washed over me. It was as if everything had finally fallen into place. I solemnly committed to no longer allowing negative influences to rule my life. I resolved to take control of my experiences, infusing them with love, persistence, and joy. I was determined to shape my future, filling it with as many moments of happiness as human existence allowed. If only I could maintain this state of bliss and sustain the level of control needed to be at my best.

Order

Fast forward to a remarkable Christmas when Hamish and Andy played hide-and-seek, and the Violet of the Dusk filled the air with beautiful music. She shared captivating stories with me and discussed the enchantment of imagination. It was a time of joy, connection, and profound beauty. Then, fast forward to a special day when the Goddess joined my wonderful extended family. We indulged in delicious food, enjoyed great company, and shared much laughter. As I left my old home that day, I was filled with vibrancy, a sense of being alive, and boundless joy, ready to embrace my new life with enthusiasm and a fresh, positive perspective.

Several wonderful days passed until the Goddess sat with me to create the Wellness Revolution website. Drawing on her profound understanding of Catholic Theology, she suggested using "We" rather than "I" when addressing various topics. This subtle yet powerful shift reframed everything. It was no longer about "me" but "us." She had already provided valuable advice to replace "God" with "Higher Power," a change that made the message more universal and relatable to a broader audience. This was a revelation for me because I had always aimed to detach my message from "me" to avoid being solely responsible for the consequences of my writing. It was not about "me" anymore but about "us."

"I" had been liberated, transformed into "We." It occurred to me that by establishing an organisation, we could create a "platform" focused not on a single individual but on the collective wisdom of all. It could serve as a medium for generating solutions that would benefit all humanity for future generations. I began to envision it as something akin to a "Messiah," not a singular human figure, but rather a divine force capable of transcending human limitations, helping us rediscover the essence of "God" and our collective potential. As this realisation set in, I drifted into a peaceful sleep, freed from having my ideas tied solely to "me." It was a profound relief, and in my slumber, I contemplated numerous groundbreaking ideas, awakening early the next morning to compose a work I titled *Perfect Order*.

"Many great religious texts speak of an order, a guiding principle that provides purpose and meaning. To me, this order is the unwavering certainty of our path, both as individuals and as a collective, encompassing our roles within our communities, nations, and the natural laws that govern and steer the actions of our planet, the Milky Way, our galaxy, and the vast expanse of the universe beyond."

Looking back, I realise it was far from perfect, but in my manic state, it felt that way. Yet, once again, I was shut down. Despite the considerable effort I had poured into it, she showed no willingness even to take a look, passing judgment on a book before it could be read. All because I had chosen to name my business "Messiah." It might not have been the best choice, but it felt perfect. So, I lost control. I impulsively gathered all my belongings and angrily stormed out, driving home in a rage. *Perfect Order* was a collection of ideas gathered over several years, summarised precisely in approximately 15 minutes:

"The universe's origin can be traced back to a simple particle existing in isolation. Under the influence of the strong force, these particles began to split and transform, giving rise to the first and most rudimentary fields. While the intricate details of this transformation are best left to the distinguished minds of quantum physics, these fields orchestrated the alignment of fundamental particles into protons, neutrons, and other nucleic particles, ultimately forming nuclei. The weak magnetic force then played its role, generating radiation that extended in all directions, shaping the electromagnetic field that brought electrons into orbit within their atomic clouds. This arrangement allowed electrons to exist simultaneously everywhere and in every state, an underlying perfect order within the atom. It is only when atoms are subjected to various forms of stress that electrons are released from their orbits, creating the phenomenon we know as electricity. These liberated electrons connect atoms, leading to the extraordinary power evident in processes like fusion and fission reactions within the sun, which manifests as energy in the form of light across the electromagnetic spectrum.

As atoms adopted this perfect order of light, electrons began to exchange, forming the foundation of our chemistry. Chemistry, at its core, is the exchange of different forms of electrons stabilised through various chemical bonds. This process enables metabolism, facilitating chemical interactions and exchanges, ultimately shaping the perfect chemistry order. Detailed insights into these interactions can be found in chemical databases compiled by the world's foremost chemists, encompassing fascinating phenomena like the behaviour of acids and bases.

The collaborative effort of chemicals and atoms results in the existence of matter in its diverse states, plasma, solids, liquids, gases, and beyond. This chemical evolution gives rise to various substances, including those integral to Earth's composition: land (minerals and rocks), sea (salt and water), and sky (atmosphere and air). This progression laid the foundation for the emergence of life through the intricate interplay of viruses, RNA, DNA, ribosomes, and other fundamental components of cellular structure. The evolution of life saw the proliferation of bacteria, initially populating the oceans before expanding to colonise the entire Earth, from the land to the sky. Plants and animals followed suit, and ultimately, humanity emerged.

Humanity's journey led to the forming of communities, villages, towns, and eventually cities. As human beings united under the banner of common humanity, various world religions played a unifying role alongside the explorations of conquerors and the rise and fall of empires. The objective exchange of currency furthered this unity. Now, human beings find themselves on a quest for a shared agenda and purpose, culminating in the unification of cultures, languages, technologies, and the human species through an era of collaboration among experts and the standardisation of technology and business processes.

This collective effort will pave the way for creating systems, policies, and legislation based on the principles of humanity, including ethics, morality, tradition, and the laws of nature. These systems will be designed to develop ideal societies through a systematic literature review, drawing from scriptures, philosophies, and scientific principles. The best evidence will be integrated with best practices, systematically implemented into human lifestyles, infrastructure, and living conditions. A global literature review, demographic analysis, input-output mapping, and the development of cutting-edge digital and engagement platforms will facilitate this process, captivating and inspiring all who partake. Ultimately, there will be no doubt, only complete certainty that perfect order will be achieved."

Crisis

The Day of My Creation

A few days passed without any special occasion. Still, on an ordinary day, I felt an inexplicable urge to embark on my own Creation Story, a narrative I had nurtured for years, rich with knowledge about the creation of the universe and evolution. I had always dreamed of living out the Seven Days of Creation each day, and it felt as if this moment was the perfect opportunity to manifest that dream. In my mind, this day marked the Day of My Creation.

I drove to JB Hi-Fi to gather the technology I needed to share my story in various forms, print, podcasts, vlogs, blogs, and audiobooks. I spent over $2,500 on a GoPro for filming, a drone for breathtaking aerial shots, a podcasting kit, and a screen for versatile filming backgrounds. I selected cutting-edge technology, and a helpful staff member guided me through the purchase. A quick transfer at the counter, a swipe of my card, and it was done. I was now equipped to begin weaving my narrative.

On the way to Seven Hills, I stopped at Wall Park Avenue, deciding not to risk using my phone while driving. There, I arrived unexpectedly at the home of my Gift Seeker, who was not anticipating my visit. I loved surprising my friends, especially when it made them feel special.

I began drafting a script for the occasion, telling the Gift Seeker that it might not make sense initially, but it would soon enough. Kneeling before her, I said, "My Gift Seeker, will you marry me?" She nearly collapsed in surprise, but I quickly added, "Just kidding." We shared a laugh before I launched into the story. I spoke of her beautiful soul, pure heart, and inability to lie. I shared how I had recognised her talent and how, with the right support, she had found her tribe. Her journey not only boosted my confidence but also helped me find myself as well. I expressed my deepest gratitude for her and concluded, "Now, let me show you the gifts I possess."

I guided her into a trance, hoping to open her mind to the unfolding narrative. “Close your eyes,” I said, “and visualise all your dreams coming true, and then some. You are a vital part of this story.” I paused momentarily before continuing, “Now, imagine the world you want to wake up to tomorrow. Take my hand and let us go for a ride.”

We set off on a car journey, passing by One Door, where I explained the Visionless Leader’s role as the story’s antagonist, leading people astray. We discussed our destination as we drove, sharing a meal and enjoying a cumquat iced tea.

The unfolded story was a tapestry of incredible proportions, a fantasy filled with magic, mystery, monsters, villains, and a touch of tragedy, just enough to keep the ending tantalisingly out of reach. It unfolded with suspense, each sentence punctuated with exclamation marks and full stops, carefully structured to maintain the narrative’s rhythm. There were elements of Shakespearean drama intertwined with the enchanting charm of Harry Potter. The tale explored themes of religion, evolution, and science, but above all, it was marked by an overwhelming sense of mystery and fun, offering a rollercoaster of emotions. We felt like joyful children, skipping along with abandon as if the world around us had vanished and we were invisible, lost in our little universe.

As the story climaxed, we decided to head back home, knowing that the adventure would continue another day. In my manic state, the Great Story had led the Gift Seeker on a journey that began with surprise, evolved into a suspenseful narrative, and reached a thrilling climax, touching on elements of fantasy, mystery, and a unique form of tragedy. It was a Disney-like tale, in which even the villain found happiness.

The Gift Seeker remained suspended in the story, emotions swirling like the tides of an ocean. I had become the Great Storyteller, recounting the tale of evolution. This journey began with an exploration of the best that the physical world had to offer, cutting-edge technology. This technology had propelled humanity to the moon, but also held the power to threaten our existence when misused. On the first day of the Evolution Story, the Great Storyteller soared to the moon in a manic state, and it would take many substances to bring him back to Earth. He would remain immersed in his story, far removed from the "sane" and balanced reality.

People of the Earth

Day two began much like any other, devoid of grand spectacles, just another ordinary day, yet it carried a profound weight in the ongoing story. I picked up my friend, helped her into the car, and secured her wheelchair before setting off toward Seven Hills. As we drove, I could feel the subtle tension in the air. Like every day, today was imbued with the promise of another adventure. The Gift Seeker had just woken, and though her surprise was evident, her eagerness for what lay ahead was undeniable. After ensuring that Buddy, her loyal companion, had been fed, we embarked on a journey filled with wonder, mystery, and a sense of unfolding destiny.

Our first stop was Westfields, where the Gift Seeker and my friend took a quick bathroom break. Knowing the task might take some time, I gathered provisions for the day: fresh fruit juices, Subway sandwiches, a fruit salad, and several books I planned to dive into later. With everything in hand, my business goals still lingered in my mind. I had big plans to get things rolling, but my business partner's lack of response threw a wrench into those aspirations, leaving me frustrated yet determined.

The second day of our journey unfolded with the story of humanity's existence on Earth. It centred on a war between the Heavens (Sky) and the Earth (Rocks), in which exploiting the Earth's resources to fuel the Sky's needs put the planet's delicate ecological balance at risk. My mind, already fraught with paranoia, became consumed with the notion that humanity's survival hung by a thread. I felt as if we were living in what I perceived as the final days, and the weight of that belief gnawed at me all afternoon.

Feeling a deep sense of urgency, I knew I had to reach out to the world's technological leaders. With this, I drafted an email to Elon Musk, one I intended to send the following morning. In it, I outlined a vision for a new era of collaboration, where the world's greatest minds and most influential business leaders would unite their resources. I named this ambitious project Messiah, believing it would offer salvation for humanity:

"You are vital to our narrative. Ever wonder why? Because the state we find ourselves in is the culmination of our collective egos. We must come together to address our challenges, offering the best of our exceptional minds and technologies.

The world is awakening to the dawn of 'We.' I play a significant role in our transformation into 'We,' but I do not possess all the answers yet. Do not let it overwhelm you. Remember, there is no 'I' in 'Us.' I exist. But 'We' must hold no grudges to extend forgiveness. 'We' love 'You,' and the future of our planet lies within your hands.

Now, back to the point...

The conflict between Heaven and Earth is endangering our species' future. If the great Goddess is to survive, she must embrace an era of collaboration, using Her technology for the greater good while establishing regulations. When you awaken, Goddess, relinquish your ego. You cannot do this alone. Technology alone will not suffice. 'We,' representing Heaven and Earth, must jointly shape the planet's destiny; otherwise, there will be no 'forever.'"

Prepare for a new reality when you awaken. Failure to change could result in us losing you to God forever. You may consider me self-centred, but I implore your forgiveness as the planet's fate hangs in the balance. You have not lost God, but 'We' must seek Him out. God is the architect of this story, and I promise to find Him, but 'We' are crucial to this journey. It will make sense in the end. It will be enjoyable, provided you are prepared and possess a good sense of humour. Only by coming together in peace can 'We' overcome our inner turmoil. This journey is about resolving the conflicts deep within us, often intergenerational, even spanning past lives. It will be turbulent, but it will breathe life into the narrative. Through shared purpose and aligned agendas, 'May Peace Be Here on Earth.'

Inhabitants of Earth...

You must unite to ensure that Heaven (The Atmosphere) and Earth (The Land) do not jeopardise the future of the Great Goddess. Cease plundering the Earth to feed the Sky. Must I spell it out for you? STOP MINING THE PLANET, OR WE WILL DESTROY IT FOREVER.

'We' must assemble the finest minds and employ our technology for the benefit of all. Allow Earth to breathe. The solutions are within reach, right before our eyes. Resistance will come from authorities, and conflicts between Heaven and Earth will persist. 'You' will propel 'Us' into the Sky, and 'I' will return to reveal the story's conclusion.

Do not, for heaven's sake, ruin this. We possess only one Earth. True collaboration is the key to the planet's future and its salvation. Oh, citizens of Earth, decipher the data on my computer, or 'We' may never find God again. I vow to return once the story is complete. Seek answers from the storytellers. All will converge into one."

My brother, Philby, hastened me to sleep. It was nearly midnight when I completed the email. Sleep had become scarce, but it felt like part of the story. On Day One, the physical world was explored, and The Great Storyteller soared to the moon with the technology I had purchased. The solution to our problems lay in bringing The Great Storyteller "back to Earth", through medicine and technology, so that I could be "I" again.

Day Two marked a shift. It was no longer about "I" but about "we". Mass collaboration was the answer to the Earth's woes. By overcoming self-absorbed actions like mining and embracing a collective approach, the transformation from "I" to "we" became our path to saving the planet.

"Day One" explored the individualistic pursuit of progress, illustrated by the journey to the moon through advanced technology. It was a metaphor for a solitary approach to problem-solving. However, this journey led to the realisation that returning "to Earth", to humility and groundedness, was essential. Day Two, in contrast, embraced the collective, showing that working together as "we" was the only way to solve the Earth's crises. By embracing mass collaboration, we could overcome the destructive patterns of the past and begin healing the planet.

Bringing Life to The Story

Day 3 of the story should have been an exciting chapter, but it became a blur. I spent most of the day pacing around my hometown, lost in thought, trying to evolve the narrative. Time seemed to slip away, and the complexities of how primitive prokaryotic bacterial cells formed from inorganic chemicals, RNA, and eventually DNA felt too intricate to delve into for this story.

The details are hazy now, but I recall wandering around the block, a comical incident at the pub when I asked for water, and meeting some random people. When I returned home, I found Mother Dearest and my brother Philby assembling a bookshelf. Philby shared a book he liked, but the rest of the day was spent pacing under the scorching sun, weaving together thousands of story threads in my mind, like a director overseeing different film frames. Lucky, a key character in the narrative, occasionally appeared, but I often zoned in and out of various realities, as any good storyteller might.

As the afternoon wore on, I attempted to set up my drone, piecing together my understanding of a higher power. My focus was on breathing life into the story. Hours passed in prayer, reflection, and deep contemplation on a profound idea related to realism, a perspective that I felt could bring much-needed balance to our beloved Goddess Earth.

"It is not idealism, but realism. Realism is born through countless prayers, acceptance, non-attachment, and faith in the unknown. It requires a life of preparation, exploring a diversity of religious and philosophical worldviews, and the humble acceptance of a higher power."

This higher power, I believed, was the mystical, psychic, and spiritual energy that balances our souls, both in this life on Earth and through reincarnation in the afterlife. To free our souls into the afterlife, we must first find peace in the rhythms of daily life. This involves understanding the ecological balance of our planet, the sea, the sky, and the earth, and how fragile this balance is. The climate is far from stable, and we must adjust our lifestyles and living conditions to honour this higher power.

"We must align ourselves, our families, communities, nations, and the global society with a unified purpose. A purpose that can bring harmony to our Earth, Goddess, Gaia, and Pachamama."

"We" can prepare for well-being by living in balance with this higher power and helping restore balance to our Goddess Earth. But first, we must confront our traumas, our own, our families', our communities', our nations', and even the Earth's. These are not your fault; they result from the fall caused by our sins."

To restore balance, we must reclaim power from our traumas. To free ourselves from them, we need to detach from our culture and avoid becoming overly attached to any one religion or philosophy. This allows for a balanced perspective that explores scientific evidence, diverse academic disciplines, religious scriptures, and best practices in human affairs. This is not a process of discarding belief but finding unity through diversity, through a spectrum of thought. And through it all, one must maintain a good sense of humour.

"Acceptance of a higher power and the ability to live in balance within body, mind, and spirit, only then can we regain control over our struggles. Only then can we start healing ourselves, restoring ethical perspectives and morality, healing others, and sharing love with the planet and the universe?"

You must direct your intention towards healing, love, and true synchronicity. Then, you will learn true magic, the ability to direct your will, life force, desire, and purpose in a controlled manner. Only then will you begin to restore balance and understand what true health and happiness mean in yourself and the universe. Only then can you devise a genuine business plan for investing in yourself, your family, your community, and your nation, bringing true peace to the people of the Earth.

When you wake up, ask yourself, “How am I feeling today? What is my higher power telling me this morning? Am I ready to believe that anything is possible today?” The future of humanity might depend on your answer. Is humanity prepared, or must we usher in a New Day? Are you ready today?

At that moment, I realised how alone I was. I believed I could solve the world’s problems, but no one seemed to share my enthusiasm. I contacted several friends for help setting up my drone and getting the technology ready, but everyone was busy with their own things, unwilling to stop what they were doing to help. I asked people on the street, but no one seemed interested in assisting. I wanted everything set up immediately; it was urgent. This was the Seven Days of Creation, and Day 3 was already upon us. But no one else seemed to grasp the urgency. I became anxious, feeling the weight of isolation bearing down on me.

Laying Restless in Bed

Day 4 of the Evolution Story felt like the final hours of humanity. It was a day of overwhelming paranoia and deep anxiety, a day when humankind was on the brink of extinction. As the sun set and darkness closed in, I became convinced that this was the last night for most of society. I felt as if my death was somehow intertwined with the fate of the human race and that the end of my life would somehow bring salvation. This was not just the end of my existence but the last night for countless others. The Last Day had arrived, and only a few humans would survive to usher in a 'New Dawn.'

In my fear and desperation, I turned to the Goddess of Love, thinking that if I could summon her, she might release some of the pent-up anger and frustration that had built up within her. I believed this release could bring peace of mind, not just for me, but for humanity. I called for her, hoping for divine intervention, but she was far away, spending time with her family in Queensland. I found myself sending all sorts of crude, impulsive texts, my mind spiralling into images of lust and perversion.

The night was far less dramatic than my imagination had envisioned. I lay in my bed, alone, consumed by fear and confusion. The Goddess of Love, whom I had believed could save humanity, seemed absent from the face of the Earth. In my desperate thoughts, I wondered if this was the ultimate truth: humanity, lost in its ego and desires, could not even be saved by the highest force of love. The human race seemed doomed, trapped in the last days, bound by illusions of control and self-interest. I didn't realise that lust had clouded my ego and distorted my perception. My fears had become entangled with my desires, creating confusion I could not escape.

I tossed and turned, searching for answers in the darkness. How could I prevent the calamity I feared? My friends, family, community, city, nation—everything I knew was on the verge of collapse. Everything that humanity had built, all the legacies of history, seemed destined to end. I raced, thinking, "All history has led to this moment." But even in the depths of my anxiety, I was uncertain. Was the world ready for this shift? Was I prepared to make the ultimate sacrifice for the survival of the species?

In the stillness of the night, the weight of this existential dilemma pressed down on me. The fear was suffocating, and yet there was something deeper beneath it all, something urging me to find peace, accept the uncertainty, and trust in the unknown. I didn't know how to let go of my fears or align myself with a higher purpose, but I felt that the answers lay somewhere beyond my ego, beyond the chaotic thoughts racing through my mind.

A Conversation with Wise Counsels

Amid my inner turmoil, I turned to the one person I knew who might offer guidance: Mother Dearest. She has always been a source of wisdom, providing clarity when my thoughts run wild. But when I called her, it was too late—she was asleep. Earlier that night, I had reached out to My Finest Counsel, as Mother Dearest had alerted her to my growing anxiety. It was 2:30 am, and despite the time difference, My Finest Counsel was in England, yet she answered my call, sensing the urgency of my distress.

My Finest Counsel has always been the voice of reason, the calm amidst my chaos. Yet tonight, no words could settle my turbulent mind. I was scared, confused, and unsure of what to do. My Finest Counsel believed I was sick and that my body and mind were reacting to a deeper imbalance. She thought I needed help, but who could help me? Who could help me when trapped in this web of fear and delusion? I lay in my bed, my mind spiralling, and at that moment, I felt that it was not just I who was sick—it was the Goddess herself, tangled in the same confusion and unable to free herself from the grip of her anger.

The world was nearing collapse, and no one seemed to hear my warning. Everyone dismissed my words as the ramblings of a madman. But all I wanted was to save humanity. Why couldn't they see the urgency of the moment? Why couldn't they understand the deeper, spiritual truth I felt at the core of my being?

While My Finest Counsel tried to soothe my anxiety, I grew more frustrated. In a fit of anger and despair, I threw my phone to the ground, shattering it. With it, I severed my connection to the world. The screen cracked, and my access to the comfort of information, entertainment, and external validation was gone.

I was now isolated, alone with my thoughts, and unable to retreat into the digital world for distraction. The Internet, with its infinite answers and ever-present connection to the outside world, was no longer available to me. I felt untethered, lost in a reality that seemed increasingly foreign. Little did I know, I was not only detached from the physical world but also from a balanced, "sane" reality, unable to see that my disconnection was part of a deeper spiritual transformation.

A Billion Views in a Second

I stepped onto the porch, seeking fresh air to clear my restless mind. I scrolled through Facebook absentmindedly on my laptop, a habitual distraction. Suddenly, a post caught my eye—an image of the Universe with the words, "God, take the Universe; it is yours." It had over a billion views. At that moment, a profound sense of purpose surged through me. I believed the message was meant for me, as if the Universe called me to step forward and claim my destiny. I thought, This is my moment. I am bringing forth the 'Messiah' platform. The words seemed to echo in my mind, urging me to take the entire Universe as my own.

I couldn't ignore the weight of the message. I had written a poem called 'Order' just a few days ago, and now I felt it was my responsibility to share it with the world. I posted it on Facebook, feeling that this would be my first message to the global consciousness. I believed that in this instant, the world was listening, that millions were reading my words, not billions, across the globe. My heart raced as I watched the views soar, and I believed that every person on Earth heard what I had to say.

I refreshed my feed, and another post appeared—this time, a picture of a unicorn with the words, "And as it is." This was a sign, a divine affirmation that everything was unfolding exactly as it should. The Universe was speaking directly to me through these posts.

With newfound confidence, I posted again. And again. I felt like the world responded to my thoughts and words each time. The feedback was instantaneous, as if the digital world were an extension of my mind. Every post I shared seemed to resonate, as if the collective consciousness perfectly aligned with my own. I believed I was no longer just an individual; I was the conduit through which the world was awakening.

It was magic. The connection felt so real, so profound. I was no longer just talking to myself or a small circle of friends. I was talking to the world, and the world was listening, responding, and evolving through my words. My ego swelled, believing that I held the key to global transformation and that every post I made contributed to humanity's collective awakening.

But deep down, I didn't realise that this was an illusion, a fleeting glimpse of the ego's desire for validation, a momentary glimpse of the power it craves. What I believed was an awakening was, in fact, the amplification of my ego, still attached to the idea of control, recognition, and influence.

I thought I had the world in my hands, but I had merely glimpsed the workings of the mind, a mind that had not yet learned to transcend itself.

My Last Breath

I went to bed that night with a sense of fulfilment, believing that everyone was listening to my words. For the first time, I felt I was truly living my purpose, the reason I had been born into this world. Yet, beneath the satisfaction, there lingered a gnawing fear. I was convinced that we were in the last days, that this was the end of civilisation as we knew it. It felt as though my own life would be the final act, my last breath, the catalyst for humanity's salvation.

As I lay there, restless, a strange stillness began to wash over me. I tried to hold my breath, believing my final exhale would somehow hold the key to saving the world. I took a deep breath—once, twice, three times—but it felt unnatural, impossible. Why was it so difficult to surrender to this? How did Jesus do it? How did he embrace death, knowing it was the beginning of something greater?

A rush of frustration overwhelmed me. Fuck human beings! Fuck Jesus Christ! I thought. I want to sleep. I'll deal with this later. I'll figure out the fate of humanity tomorrow. The weight of the world, the urgency of the cosmic drama I had felt earlier, suddenly seemed too heavy to bear. Surely, the survival of the human race couldn't depend on just one person. I was not the saviour of humanity. It wasn't my responsibility.

With a deep sigh, I resolved to let go of the world's fate. I was tired. I needed rest. Fuck it all, I thought, as I reached for the bottle of Seroquel. The relief of sleep beckoned, promising escape from the chaos in my mind. As the medication took hold, the tension melted away, and I finally slipped into sleep, breaking the cycle of insomnia that had plagued me for weeks.

Waking Up to A New Dawn

As the sun rose, I awoke to a profound revelation: I didn't need to die for the human race. I was, in fact, the creator of my own story—the Creator of my story, the Story. I realised I was the Creator of the Creation Story, holding the power to change the narrative of the universe's evolution forever.

As I woke to this New Dawn, I believed the 'New Earth' had always been here. All that was needed was for us to surrender to the higher power—the same force that had brought 'life' to the story the day before. I wrote:

"The reality is that when you no longer need what the Ego provides, you free it. By feeding it nothing, you receive everything. We can free ourselves from our God Delusions if we realise that we always were, are, and will be human. By surrendering to your higher power, whatever that is for you, 'I' can become 'We.' You have the power to create a Heaven here on Earth.

This realisation made me feel less alone, more connected to 'all' of creation, and to all the moments that have led up to 'now.'"

I realised that 'I' cannot exist without 'You.' We cannot create heaven on Earth alone. No one person can do it, but together, we can create a utopia. It's not enough to have a good relationship or family. We can't achieve it by working a job without knowing what we're doing day to day, our role, or how it fits into the bigger picture.

No merger between companies can solve the problems they're trying to address unless they combine the elements that allow both to thrive. No nation, religion, or race can achieve this without understanding each other's cultures, traditions, rituals, myths, history, and institutions. No politician, lawyer, or policymaker can create policies and laws that work for everyone without consulting the people whose lifestyles shape their society.

Human beings cannot exist peacefully on this planet without removing the borders—whether legal, territorial, or cultural—that divide us. No market is truly free, for it cannot control our free will. All human rights are fundamental to our well-being. We deserve free access to everything. We must express our fundamental freedoms to free ourselves from poverty, discrimination, and all forces that limit us.

We cannot exist in isolation. In unity, we free ourselves from the illusion of 'us' versus 'them.' We need to usher in an age of collaboration and imagine an ideal future where the best minds combine their resources for the benefit of all. By discovering what we already have, we can design, deliver, and develop a society that aligns with our higher values.

We are fighting against one another, entrenched in our struggles, but this power imbalance is the only thing between us and the higher power. Whether your God is God with a capital 'G,' Allah, Jah, or your own higher power, we are all one and stronger when we work together. This is how I overcame my delusion. What a profound realisation this was—freeing myself from my God Delusion. It wasn't just a belief; it was a revelation.

After waking up to my 'revelation,' I rushed to my computer and posted on my Wellness Revolution Facebook page. Continuing from the previous night's posts, I felt I was reaching billions of people with every word. I believed the world was listening to my message. I wrote:

"It's 5:49 am, 2nd January 2023. I woke up from my bed and decided to change the story of creation, evolution, and humanity today—if human beings are ready. I chose not to do it because We, Messiah, will decide how this story finishes. That right belongs to all surviving human beings on Earth by the end of today if YOU believe it is possible. So wake up, Goddess Earth!

We have a lot of work to do today to restore balance to ourselves, our communities, our cities, our nations, global society, our planet, and the ecosystem because Messiah will unravel its own story today. Through to the end of time. What is the end of time? Eternity! There is no end of time. Sorry for the rhetorical question.

Wake up, Goddess Earth. Let us work together, not against each other, and believe that creating heaven here on Earth is possible. We choose the story of evolution from here on Earth today, and it starts by asking ourselves a simple question: How do you feel today?

I will start by hearing your stories when you are ready. This is an excellent time to share a story or two. Stream a video, a movie, or a song if you like—whatever your talent is. Get up, Goddess Earth, and share your story. Email it to the Wellness Revolution, and we will try to upload it. If you believe, we can do one better. Some ingenious tech wizards, please hack the Wellness Revolution and make this an automatic process for everyone.

We need all the great minds to suspend their egos today if this will work. And that means all human beings. We all have a great mind if we learn to understand it. It can take us anywhere in the universe. All you have to do is believe. Then, like true magic, apply your will. And.... POOF! It happens.

Then, you understand what your will is. Your life force, your desire, and your intention. For centuries, mystics have seen these in our minds, the informational fields that surround and interpenetrate our bodies. We do not know it yet. Just because there have not been words yet does not mean it is impossible. It just means it has not been imagined yet. And without imagination, there can be no magic. Unfortunately, for magic to happen, you must dream big and believe it is possible. Apply discipline and concentration. And like that. POOF! Magic can happen. You have to accept it. How are you feeling now? Is the impossible possible for you yet?

So, beliefs are only our current understanding of our experience at this very moment in time, as told in our stories and cultural imprints. If you raise your understanding and awareness, you can understand my experience and find and apply genuine compassion. And that will end suffering on the planet because suffering is merely overcome through compassion.

We need to awaken this Great Goddess of ours. She does not believe yet because her understanding of herself is not ready to accept the impossible. She is stubborn. Her ego is strong. But ego stands aside with compassion, which comes with accepting and understanding your suffering. Let go of your anger, my love. Believe. Believe in life. And like magic. POOF! It can happen! You have to believe it is possible. Raise your understanding of awareness and compassion and change the planet's future. How are you feeling? Are you ready to answer that question? A simple YES, or NO?

Wake up, Goddess! Let go of your ego. Our survival on the planet depends on it. You do not know it yet. Let aside that anger. Trust me. It is not your fault. I can heal you if you are willing to trust me. You are the most incredible role model and teacher that has ever existed. Teach us. But first, you must listen to yourself. How are you feeling today?"

I genuinely believed I was broadcasting a message to everyone on the planet. I was convinced that billions of people were tuning in with each post. I thought my Messiah platform on the Wellness Revolution Facebook page had crashed Facebook and was now the only platform on the internet.

I imagined the world's tech leaders would unite to transform how people communicated and shared information. I believed that my 'Messiah platform' would change humanity's course and usher in an age of global collaboration. I thought I had launched this platform that morning.

On Day 1 of my Creation Story, the plan was to buy all the necessary technology and resources to set up the Messiah platform. I bought them and planned to work with my business partner to launch the platform. Unfortunately, my Business Partner didn't share my enthusiasm and was tired that night. But when my Business Partner showed up at 8:00 am on this 'New Dawn,' I thought it was my chance to bring my vision to life. After all, the world was tuned in for what would come.

Intervention

A New Perspective

I awoke with a sense of clarity, as if the fog that had clouded my thoughts had finally begun to lift. The air around me felt lighter, and I felt a sense of peace for the first time in a long while. My heart was filled with quiet anticipation as I thought about the possibility of speaking with a psychiatrist today. I was eager to see someone who could guide me through the maze of my mind, someone who might help me unravel the complexities that had brought me here.

Curious, I asked when I might meet with the psychiatrist. I was told it could happen anytime between 9:00 am and 3:00 pm. The uncertainty was unsettling, but I kept reminding myself that this was part of the process, a process I had to trust, even if I didn't fully understand. I hoped it would happen sooner rather than later. In the meantime, I decided to acquaint myself with the others in the ward, trying to connect in a foreign yet familiar place.

Among the people I met was Alladin. He was a gentle soul who radiated kindness despite the chaos around him. But there was a dark cloud hanging over him. A man named Black Magic had started harassing him, claiming that he had placed a $100,000 bounty on Alladin's head. The threats, though delusional, were unsettling. I soon learned that we were in the High Dependency Unit (HDU), a place for those who were considered to be at their most unstable, posing risks not only to themselves but to others as well.

As I sat with Alladin, listening to him recount the details of the threats against him, my unease grew. This was a world where reality and illusion intertwined, where kindness and cruelty existed side by side. I could feel the anxiety in the air, thick and heavy, like a storm ready to break.

Next, I spoke with the Hacker. He had been brought here after allegedly fighting back against another hacker who had tried to steal his identity. He viewed this place as a temporary inconvenience, hoping to escape by convincing the psychiatrist that his claims were merely products of his imagination. The Hacker's desperation to leave the facility was palpable, yet I could see the flicker of fear in his eyes, fear that he might never escape this place, not in the way he hoped.

I couldn't help but wonder how many of us were here for reasons not entirely our choosing, how many had been caught in the gears of a system that didn't truly understand them. Some patients, like the Hacker, might lie to escape, to regain control over their lives. I, on the other hand, could not bring myself to lie. I was here because of my truth, for better or worse. Even if it led me to places I didn't understand, honesty felt like my only lifeline.

It was then that Black Magic approached me again. His eyes, clouded with confusion and intoxication, bore into mine as he threatened me in the same way he had threatened Alladin. I breathed, grounding myself in the stillness I had found that morning. I shook my head when he asked me if I knew who he was, though I suspected where this conversation was headed.

"I am Jesus Christ," he said, his voice unwavering. "Did you know Jesus was black?"

The words were familiar to me. I had encountered similar delusions before, those whispers of grandeur that seemed to rise from the depths of the mind. But instead of dismissing him outright, I reflected on the deeper meaning of what he said. I had always believed that accepting our humanity, the beauty and the flaws, the light and the dark, was the key to understanding our divine potential.

"What if we're all in a different portal?" I asked, my voice calm. "What if we're all playing a different game? What if we're all in heaven, and we've had the potential to create heaven all along?"

Black Magic's drug-addled eyes softened for a moment, as if my words had cracked through the thick fog in his mind. For the first time in our interaction, his posture relaxed, and he introduced himself not as a figure of power but as Black Magic, a name that now seemed more a reflection of his struggle than any divine delusion.

He swore off drugs, though I knew the promise was likely to be fleeting. But for now, something had shifted. The air felt lighter between us, and I no longer saw him as a threat. He wasn't the man who would place bounties on people's heads. He was just another soul, lost in the labyrinth of his mind, seeking some semblance of peace.

I asked him how he was, and he looked me in the eye for the first time since I had met him and answered honestly, "Good."

It wasn't much, but it was enough. In a place where so many seemed to be trapped in their versions of reality, where doctors and nurses rushed by without a second thought for the emotional lives of their patients, Black Magic had broken through the barrier of fear and shared a simple truth with me.

And then, he did something that would forever shift my perspective. He hugged me, holding me tightly for a moment, and whispered, "Thank you."

At that moment, something inside me clicked. I realised that there was room for connection in this place, the High Dependency Unit, a world that was once chaotic and fragile. There was space for compassion. And for the first time in what felt like forever, I felt safe. I had found someone I could trust in a place that otherwise instilled fear.

I had entered this world uncertain, questioning everything about myself and my place there. But now, as I stood in that room, surrounded by people whose realities seemed to shift with every breath, I saw a new possibility. Perhaps this was the point at which

I could truly begin to heal, not just from the chaos around me but from the chaos within.

And perhaps, just perhaps, in this place of madness, I could find a new perspective that would allow me to see beyond the delusions and pain to a new world where anything was possible.

Trust

My conversations with Black Magic took on a new tone as the days passed. What had begun as an encounter coloured by delusions and threats slowly evolved into something more grounded. Still, I couldn't help but wonder: Was his newfound trust in me genuine, or was it merely a momentary flicker in the haze of his altered reality?

To test the boundaries of our connection, I asked him to close his eyes and allow me to "punch" him in the face. The request, playful as it seemed, was meant to challenge the nature of trust we were building. Black Magic hesitated, his mind wrestling with the idea. Finally, he nodded, albeit with visible trepidation. His cringing anticipation made me pause, but I continued with my plan.

I flicked his cheek lightly to gauge his response rather than cause harm. He flinched, his eyes opening wide in surprise, but something shifted in him, a brief moment of vulnerability, a glimpse into the fragile space where trust begins to take root.

I couldn't help but wonder: Was this test a reliable measure of trust? Was it just a whimsical game, or did it hold weight in the context of our evolving connection? It seemed too simple a test, too fleeting, to measure something as profound as trust. Yet, in that moment, it felt significant, like a bridge, however fragile, that had begun to form between us.

Later, I suggested a trust exercise that resembled the typical team-building activities I had witnessed in corporate settings. We took turns leaning back, letting the other catch us, hoping the other person would support us in the fall. I watched Black Magic's body language closely, waiting to see if his trust in me would be enough to surrender to the moment, to lean back and allow me to catch him.

As we performed the exercise, I couldn't help but question its value. Was this play a temporary bonding experience, or did it have a deeper meaning? It felt significant at the time, yet I couldn't escape the nagging feeling that the exercise didn't fully capture the complexities of trust. In these simple actions, was I truly seeing the essence of trust, or was it a superficial show of confidence that would fade once the moment passed?

That evening, I repeated the exercise with my Best Friend. There was a different energy between us, a history, a depth that made the moment feel more genuine. But even then, I questioned: Was this fleeting vulnerability enough to cultivate a lasting sense of safety? A single moment of shared trust could not represent the entire trust spectrum in relationships. And yet, it felt like the beginning of something meaningful.

Reflecting on these experiences, I realised that trust, while undoubtedly crucial for healing and connection, is a far more intricate concept than a few exercises or tests can reveal. Trust isn't something that can be fully measured in a moment of vulnerability, no matter how genuine. It takes time, consistency, and a willingness to show up for one another, not just in brief moments of need but through the ebb and flow of life's more complex challenges.

Trust was fragile and powerful in a place like the High Dependency Unit. It was formed in the cracks of the human experience, where the façade of our lives broke down, and we could see each other as we truly were, vulnerable, uncertain, but capable of something greater. But while trust is a cornerstone of recovery and connection, it is clear that the transient nature of these simple exercises only scratches the surface of what is required for trust to endure.

True trust, the kind that binds us and supports us through life's most difficult moments, is forged through shared experiences, consistent actions, and a willingness to risk vulnerability repeatedly. It's more than fleeting moments of support. It's the quiet knowing that, no matter what happens, we are there for each other. And perhaps that is where true trust begins, not in the test of a single moment, but in the ongoing dance between hearts that choose to lean on one another.

You cannot prove trust through an exercise or a playful game. It is built when you least expect it, when the stakes are high, and when the world around you feels uncertain. Trust is the space between two people where both choose to be vulnerable, to offer their hearts without reservation. It's a choice that lasts long after the exercise ends and echoes through every interaction, decision, and act of compassion.

And so, while I had found trust in Black Magic, I understood that it was just the beginning. Trust would be tested repeatedly amid shifting realities and fragile minds in this space. But perhaps that was the point, to discover the depth of trust not through games or exercises but through being present, through leaning into each other and knowing that, in the end, we could catch one another.

Rights

The hospital walls felt more suffocating with each passing hour, and I grew increasingly frustrated as I waited for the psychiatrist who was supposed to begin my treatment plan. The anticipation was starting to feel like a slow burn. But my frustration deepened when Black Magic told me he hadn't seen a doctor or psychiatrist in six days. Then the Hacker, who had been at the hospital for an extended period, shared something that would change my perspective on the situation, our patient rights.

He explained that, according to hospital regulations, patients should be seen by medical personnel within 12 hours of admission. The weight of this statement hit me hard. I had already been here for over five hours, passed through the Triage and Assessment Centre (TAC) for a brief evaluation, and then spent an uncomfortable night in the emergency department. I was told I would be seen in the morning, but that turned into before lunch. Hours passed, and still, no psychiatrist came. Eventually, I was transferred to the High Dependency Unit (HDU) and told I would be seen in the morning, only to hear later that it might not be until 3:00 pm.

It was disheartening. The Hacker's account of his two-week stay, coupled with Black Magic's six-day wait, only amplified my unease. Something was wrong here.

That's when the Hacker brought up the Rights Statement, a document I had been advocating for that should have been handed to every patient upon admission. Yet, somehow, it had never been given to me. The Hacker retrieved his copy and handed it over for me to read, but with the condition that I return it afterwards, since he needed it to fight for his rights.

The Rights Statement was a clear, firm declaration of patient rights. It defined the difference between a "mentally ill" person and a "mentally disordered" person, a distinction that would have been important for anyone trying to navigate their care. The document stipulated that patients had the right to see medical personnel no later than 12 hours after entering the facility and that a patient, or someone on their behalf, could request to see the Medical Superintendent at any time for release. It also highlighted that patients should be assessed by a medical specialist every 24 hours.

But there was a problem. I had been in the hospital for over 48 hours and still hadn't seen any medical personnel. Black Magic, who had been here for six days, was in the same boat. None of us had been properly assessed, either subjectively or objectively, as a "mentally ill" person. This was not just a medical oversight but a violation of our rights.

I felt a surge of indignation. I demanded to see the Medical Superintendent, invoking the right explicitly stated in the Rights Statement. I wasn't just a patient anymore. I was a person with rights and determined to assert them.

I was told to put my request in writing. It seemed that the medical superintendent was incredibly busy and would likely not respond until the following Wednesday or Thursday. This was Thursday, and I wasn't sure I could wait that long.

The nurses, seemingly indifferent to the urgency of my request, explained that I could express my concerns through the Official Visitors box, where I could lodge a complaint or provide feedback, positive or negative. Official Visitors, they said, came once a month. And, as if by some cosmic joke, they were due to arrive that very afternoon.

The irony wasn't lost on me. Here I was, a patient in urgent need of care, forced to wait for a system that had already failed me. Yet, simultaneously, I couldn't help but wonder if this moment of frustration would catalyse change, if asserting our rights, speaking up, and demanding the care we were entitled to would make a difference.

As I sat there, waiting for the Official Visitors to arrive, I reflected on what it meant to truly be heard in a system that often overlooked the rights of those most vulnerable. My frustration was compounded by the realisation that, as patients, we were usually treated as passive recipients of care rather than active participants in our healing. The waiting game felt endless, and each moment spent in this system felt like a small erosion of my autonomy and dignity.

But even in this helpless moment, I knew I had a choice, to remain silent and endure, or to speak up, claim my rights, and push back against a system that had let me, and so many others, down. While the road to being heard was not easy, this moment reminded me of how essential it was to stand firm in the face of systemic indifference, no matter how daunting it seemed.

In the end, perhaps the greatest right we have as individuals, especially in moments of vulnerability, is the right to be treated with dignity, to be seen and heard, and to assert our humanity in spaces that often try to erase it. My journey through this hospital was far from over, but I had already learned one thing. Rights are only meaningful when they are actively claimed, and no one, not even a system built to care for the most vulnerable, could take that away from me.

Asking To Speak to The Medical Superintendent

On January 3rd, 2023, at approximately 4:30 pm, I was brought to the High Dependency Unit. I had been waiting for more than 23 hours without seeing a doctor, despite the clear stipulation in the Rights Statement I had reviewed, which states that I should be seen by a facility doctor no later than 12 hours after arriving at a mental health facility. This was a breach of my rights, a fact that weighed heavily on my mind as I sat there, trying to remain calm.

When I first arrived, I was told I would see a doctor. So, I waited overnight, expecting my concerns to be addressed the following day. But the hours stretched on, and when I was told that I would be seen no later than 3:00 pm, I thought surely this would be the moment my care would finally begin. But when the clock struck 3:00 pm, I asked the nurse why there had been such a delay. The response I received was dismissive, almost contemptuous: "Doctors don't run at that time."

I felt my frustration rising as I responded, "It's the law; are doctors not bound by it?" The nurse didn't answer. Instead, he shut the door in my face.

This was not just about my health anymore, but my rights. This was about being treated with dignity and respect, and I felt I had been neither seen nor heard. I spent the night stewing in anger, disappointment, and helplessness. I knew that I was not well, but I also knew that I had the right to be treated with care and respect while I sought to get well.

When I woke up the next morning, I reviewed the Rights Statement again, particularly the part that stated, "I may, at any time, ask the medical superintendent or another authorised medical officer to let me out." This was my right, and it became clear that I had to exercise it. If I couldn't get the care I needed here, I had every right to ask to be transferred to a facility that could provide it.

I decided to call Law Access NSW, hoping for some guidance on how to move forward. Unfortunately, they couldn't provide legal advice, but they did give me three numbers to call. I called each number one by one, hoping to find someone who could advocate for me or, at the very least, help me understand my options. As I dialled the last number, I only wanted to speak to someone who could ensure I received the care I was entitled to. I didn't need to be given legal counsel. I just wanted to be treated fairly and appropriately.

In my heart, I knew I wasn't "well," but I also knew I needed to be in the right place to heal. I had been to Ramsey Clinic before, and their care had always been exemplary. I was not seeking to escape. I was seeking the best care possible, and I believed that was at Ramsey. I needed to be in a facility where I felt safe, respected, and capable of healing. But for that to happen, I needed to ensure my rights were upheld, and I needed the support of the Medical Superintendent to advocate for my wellbeing.

I knew the staff were busy, and I understood the daily challenges, but this was more than just a matter of convenience or resources. It was about my human dignity and my right to appropriate care. As I prepared to request a meeting with the Medical Superintendent, I decided to take further action. I would continue to push for the care I deserved, not just for myself but for anyone else who might find themselves in this situation, overlooked and disregarded.

I knew this process might take time and require legal intervention, but I was prepared to follow through. I clearly understood my rights and wouldn't let this system dismiss them any longer. If I had to seek legal advice or escalate my concerns to a higher authority, I would do so. My rights were being breached, and I would no longer be silent.

At that moment, I knew that asserting my rights was not just about seeking treatment. It was about reclaiming my autonomy, my voice, and my place in a system that had forgotten its responsibility to its patients. My journey wasn't just about getting well. It was about ensuring that everyone in my position would be treated with the respect and care they deserved, regardless of their condition.

I hoped, more than anything, that this would be the beginning of a change, not just for me but for others like me. And as I sat there, waiting for the Medical Superintendent's response, I realised that perhaps the real work, the real healing, had already begun.

Reconstruction

Good, that is The Way It Should Be

The clock struck 3:00 p.m., then 3:30 p.m., and yet there was still no sign of the doctor I had been promised. The hours went on, my frustration was growing with each passing minute. I had been told I would be seen between 3:00 and 3:30 p.m., yet there was no sign of the medical professional who was supposed to assess me. When the clock finally reached 3:30 p.m., I could no longer stay silent.

I approached the nurse and asked, "When will I see the doctor?" His response was curt and dismissive: "Psychiatrists don't run simultaneously as you." It was an answer that felt less like an explanation and more like an attempt to brush off my concerns. I had made it clear that I was aware of my rights, but his answer felt like an outright dismissal.

I pointed out, "The statement of my rights guarantees that I will see a professional within 12 hours of arriving at this facility. This is a breach of my rights."

Instead of acknowledging my concerns or reassuring me, the nurse retorted with disdain, "What makes you so important that you should see the psychiatrist when you want?" I was taken aback. My rights were clear, and yet I was being treated as though I were a nuisance, as though my need for care didn't matter.

I calmly replied, "These are my rights, the law. Are psychiatrists above the law?" I was not trying to be difficult; I was merely asserting that my rights as a patient were being ignored.

The anxiety I had been trying to keep in check must have been evident because the nurse's response seemed to grow colder. The situation was escalating, and I knew I had to remain composed. But as I explained to Black Magic about the rights statement and the illegal delay in seeing a doctor, I could sense the tension mounting. Black Magic, who had already endured a lifetime of struggles with schizophrenia, seemed just as agitated. His patience, too, was wearing thin.

Finally, after much back-and-forth, Black Magic requested to speak with a nurse about his rights. After a tense wait, the nurse emerged from his station behind the glass doors for the first time since I had arrived in the High Dependency Unit. When he spoke, it wasn't with the calm professionalism I had expected, it was with an unmistakable air of intimidation. He went through the Rights Statement with Black Magic in such a manner that it felt less like a conversation about rights and more like an interrogation.

The nurse's approach clearly shook Black Magic, already on edge. After the interaction, he confided, "Now I feel intimidated and will be scared to ask you for help." It was a painful admission, one that highlighted the profound disconnect between the supposed care he was receiving and the reality of what he was enduring.

The nurse's response to Black Magic was chilling. In a tone that dripped with authority and disdain, he said, "Good, that's how it should be."

I was seething with anger, though I kept it inside. How could anyone justify treating a patient, especially one with such a severe mental health condition, like this? Black Magic was already facing the daily challenge of living with schizophrenia, and now he was subjected to an environment that seemed designed to exacerbate his suffering. How could someone tasked with providing care, someone who was supposed to be there to help, use fear and intimidation as tools of "care"?

The entire exchange left me questioning the very nature of the institution I had entered. The nurse's behaviour wasn't an isolated incident but part of a larger pattern of disregard for the patient's dignity and rights. This wasn't about providing treatment or creating an environment conducive to healing. It was about control, about maintaining a sense of power over people who were already vulnerable.

For the rest of my stay in the High Dependency Unit, I never saw that nurse step out from behind the glass again. He didn't show any support or gave any guidance during my time there, and his behaviour left me wondering about his motivations. Why choose a profession centred around care and healing if your approach to helping people was to make them feel small, intimidated, and powerless?

I couldn't understand it. How could someone who worked in a place meant for healing be so detached from the essence of care? Was it possible to become so jaded, so disillusioned with your role, that you lost sight of the humanity in those you were meant to serve? The nurse's actions were a stark reminder of how the system failed those within it. It wasn't just the delay in treatment that was troubling, it was the toxic culture that allowed for dehumanising treatment to occur unchecked.

At that moment, I knew I had to fight for my rights. Not just for my own sake but for Black Magic and anyone else trapped in this system. It wasn't enough to silently accept what was happening. We needed to make our voices heard, demand accountability, and ensure that our rights were respected in theory and practice.

The nurse's chilling words, "Good, that's how it should be," would stay with me, a haunting reminder of the importance of standing up and speaking out, even when the system seems determined to silence you.

Official Visitors

I have always held a deep respect for the Official Visitors Program. I had even applied to work for them, believing in the power of advocacy and change. In a similar role at St John of God Hospital, I joined the Consumer Advisory Partners Committee (CAPC). Our role was to collect patient feedback, escalate concerns to the executive committee, and ultimately drive the positive changes needed in the hospital. Our efforts made significant strides in ensuring open communication between patients and the hospital's decision-makers. Much like the work I did at St John of God, this program was built on a simple but powerful principle: ensuring that patients' voices were heard and respected.

Official Visitors perform a similar advocacy role across New South Wales. They are tasked with ensuring that mental health services meet patients' needs while adhering to the rights, laws, and standards set in place to protect vulnerable individuals. These visitors act as a bridge between the hospital and the community, advocating for change at both the service and system levels. I admired their role and hoped their presence would bring about some much-needed change in the environment I found myself in.

On the verge of losing my composure, I approached one of the nursing staff and asked when the Official Visitors would be arriving. The frustration and anxiety that had been building up inside me felt unbearable, and I was desperate for some form of validation or resolution. To my surprise, a man and woman with gentle smiles turned to me and said, "We are the Official Visitors." My heart lifted slightly, knowing that at least someone was here who might be able to help.

I wrote my complaints on paper and placed them in the Official Visitor feedback box. However, the key the hospital provided didn't work, and I couldn't access the box to deliver my concerns. When the Official Visitors arrived and asked if they could discuss my grievances, I welcomed the opportunity. This was the moment I had been waiting for, the chance to voice my concerns in a way that might lead to real change.

We sat together for 30–40 minutes and gently addressed my concerns. I explained that my rights and the rights of other patients had been violated, referencing the statement of rights that outlined the legal guarantees we were entitled to. I mentioned that a fellow patient had felt intimidated when inquiring about their rights and that I had repeatedly raised concerns with the staff about the Partners in Consumer Standards, as highlighted by the Australian Commission on Safety and Quality in Health Care.

I calmly explained that if patients' rights weren't respected, how could we expect to get "well"? How could we improve in an environment where the staff seemed content to intimidate and dismiss us? It was hard to reconcile the idea of healing with the harsh reality of the environment around us. How could we be expected to trust the system when it seemed so intent on failing us?

The Official Visitors took the time to listen attentively, asking thoughtful questions. They inquired about the nurse who had intimidated Black Magic, but unfortunately, he was on a break. Despite this, the conversation continued in a supportive and validating manner. I felt connected and understood as I shared more about my advocacy work for this hospital, the Primary Health Network (PHN), and the Global Mental Health Peer Network (GMHPN). The Official Visitors and the PHN and GMHPN representatives thanked me for my efforts and assured me that my concerns would not go unheard. They validated my feelings and reinforced that they would do everything possible to ensure the hospital recognised the importance of adhering to patient rights, laws, and standards.

For the first time in days, I felt a sense of peace. I felt heard, understood, and supported. The Official Visitors made it clear that they would work to improve the facility, not just for me but for all patients in similar situations. This was a moment of true advocacy, where the patients' voices were acknowledged and taken seriously by those in positions to effect change.

The conversation with the Official Visitors gave me the peace of mind I desperately sought. It wasn't just about my situation, but the systemic change needed for everyone in this facility and beyond. It was a reminder that, even in the darkest times, some people would fight for what was right and stand up for us when the system failed.

This conversation didn't erase the trauma I had experienced, but it did offer a glimmer of hope that change was possible, that, despite the flaws in the system, some cared enough to challenge it and make it better. It gave me the strength to continue fighting, not just for my recovery but for the rights of every person who walked through those hospital doors.

Andrew Turtle

Unofficial Visitor

I had been reassured repeatedly that I was in the best place to get better, but when I was told I had a visitor, my heart raced with anticipation. I had expected my best friend to visit after work, after 6:00 p.m. Who could it be? I wondered. Then, as though an angel had entered the room, the Black Priest walked in, his presence enveloping me with warmth and light.

The Black Priest had brought me a bottle of coconut water, saying his mother, my Great Friend, had told him I had mentioned wanting it as a treat. Asking for a cup to share the delicacy, we poured glasses and savoured every sip. The simple act of sharing coconut water felt like a profound gesture of care and connection.

The Black Priest has been a significant figure in my life, though his mother, my Great Friend, holds an even deeper place in my heart. I once lived in her caravan, helped her tell the first 20 years of her story, and shared countless adventures. Their family had embraced me during Christmas festivities in years past, though I missed joining them this year. It was a regret that weighed heavily on me, as his wife and children always made me feel welcome.

While the Black Priest and I had been childhood friends, we weren't particularly close as adults. His visit surprised me, especially knowing he didn't have a driver's licence then. Seeing his larger, less athletic frame was a stark contrast to the elite swimmer he once was, having broken some of Ian Thorpe's records during training. Life had changed for him, softened by a good Mormon life and a wife who lovingly spoiled him in every way.

When he greeted me with a simple "Hi," I didn't anticipate the depth of our conversation. Somehow, I found myself disclosing secrets I had buried for years, ones I had only ever shared with two people. Not even his mother, who knew almost everything about me, had heard these truths.

"Do you remember the school camp we went on as kids?" I asked.

"Yes," he replied. "I remember having to bring your Powerade because you were so dehydrated."

"Do you remember why I was dehydrated?" I pressed.

"The teachers said you hadn't drunk enough water on such a hot day," he responded.

"Did you know our Jealous Friend spiked my drink with some sort of drug?" I revealed.

"No, I didn't," he said, his voice tinged with concern.

"Do you remember me rowing like crazy in the canoe with you and Bergan?"

"Yes," he said. "Even I couldn't keep up."

"Did you know I was raped?" I blurted out.

There was a long pause. I couldn't believe the words had escaped my lips. I had never shared this with another man. Like his mother's, his eyes gazed into mine with deep compassion.

"I'm sorry," he said softly. "I didn't know. I'm so sorry you had to go through that."

Relief coursed through me. For the first time, I felt a weight lift; the shame and humiliation that had held me captive for so long started to dissipate. Saying it aloud to someone who responded with such empathy was empowering. Whether or not the assault had occurred, the fear and trauma had been real for me, and now I no longer had to carry it alone. I could reclaim some of the control that had been taken from me.

After that, our conversation flowed effortlessly. It was remarkable how trust could create a space for healing. We spoke about his work as a prison warden, specifically his role in delivering Dialectical Behavioural Therapy (DBT) to inmates, many of whom had borderline personality disorder (BPD) as a coping mechanism for their traumas. He noted the parallels between their struggles and those his mother had endured before finding healing through her faith in Jesus Christ and the Latter-Day Saints.

The Black Priest explained that while DBT was originally designed for individuals with BPD, its principles could benefit anyone. Rooted in Cognitive Behavioural Therapy (CBT), DBT includes strategies for improving emotional regulation, distress tolerance, and interpersonal effectiveness. He encouraged me to explore the possibility of joining a group that practised DBT, believing it could help me as well.

Although his visit was limited to 30 minutes, it was deeply impactful. Recognising my distress and the oppressive environment of the mental health ward, he shared his hope that one day, such restrictions would no longer be necessary, and everyone could experience true freedom. He even attempted to find a quote from the Book of Mormon on his phone to share but couldn't locate it in time. Still, his presence and words were enough.

Trusting the sincerity in his eyes, I felt an incredible release. A simple word, "sorry," was all the validation I needed to feel less isolated. The Black Priest's visit reminded me that moments of connection and compassion could spark healing and hope even in the darkest places.

The Medical Superintendent

Although I was informed that the superintendent might not respond to my request until the middle of the following week, my email did not go unheard. Despite the delay I had been prepared for, I was pleasantly surprised when the Medical Superintendent agreed to meet with me. It is a patient's right to request a meeting with the superintendent at any time, but the fact that he took the time to listen to me was a small yet significant act of respect.

We sat together in the courtyard for about 35 minutes, and during that time, he addressed my concerns with a genuine willingness to listen. This meeting wasn't just about protocol; it was a meaningful exchange. By the end, I felt seen, heard, and understood, a feeling that often seemed elusive in the mental health system.

The superintendent validated my efforts to advocate for myself and others, acknowledging that I had raised important points about patient care. He also provided clarity about my treatment and the policies guiding it. After our meeting, he followed up with an email summarising our discussion, documenting our conversation and reinforcing the value of consumer collaboration. The message read:

From the Medical Superintendent, Kristof Mikes-Liu:

"Thank you for your correspondence with the Medical Superintendent. We met this afternoon, and I agreed to write a summary of our discussion, which would also count as the record in your notes. I partially decided to do this because you commented that consumers should better partner with clinicians in the documentation.

There were a couple of topics we discussed:

1. You mentioned that a medical officer did not see you within 12 hours of arriving at the facility. By this, you understood the

facility to be HDU. I explained that the decision to admit you as an involuntary patient occurred while you were in the Emergency Department and that an Accredited Person reviewed you within 12 hours of this decision. We discussed how there might be a mismatch between the Rights form and the updates to the Mental Health Act.

2. You also discussed the need to be reviewed every 24 hours. I clarified that this requirement applied to persons who were admitted as Mentally Disordered persons, whereas you were accepted as a Mentally Ill person.

3. You shared that your experience at Nepean was considerably better than when you were admitted as an 18-year-old. However, you also expressed that you would recover better at Ramsay Health. You mentioned discussing some issues with the Official Visitors yesterday.

4. I conveyed that I believed your team was working to facilitate your transfer to the private facility, but they were concerned about you being well enough to go. Based on my interview today, I mentioned that you seemed better than when you arrived but still not as well as possible. You agreed with this assessment. I added that there might be differing opinions regarding when a person might be ready for transfer to a private facility. We concurred that this could be the case.

5. You spoke about your experiences with the peer movement, contributions to organisations like the PHN, and the design of this facility. You emphasised the importance of person-centred care and greater collaboration with consumers, and I expressed sympathy for your perspective."

I informed you that the team would review your suitability for transfer on Monday, and you were okay with this. I could not promise an outcome, but I trusted that the team would do its best. I mentioned that you could appeal to the Mental Health Review Tribunal, and you said you were not considering that at this stage.

"Thank you for your time today. I wish you the best for 2023 and your recovery."

The email proved his professionalism and willingness to engage with me as an equal partner in my care. I had long championed the need for collaboration between consumers and clinicians, and this interaction was a testament to how far the mental health system could go when such collaboration was embraced.

While I wasn't guaranteed an immediate solution, I was comforted by his transparency and the promise that my concerns would be taken seriously. Being listened to and respected as a human being, not just a patient, made a significant difference to my sense of dignity and hope for recovery.

The superintendent's understanding and validation reinforced an important truth: healing is not just about medical treatment, it's about feeling empowered, heard, and part of the process. At that moment, I knew my advocacy efforts for myself and others were not in vain.

You are Not My Partner

Life in the High Dependency Unit had a rhythm of its own, but for me, it felt stagnant. I worked hard to find stability amidst the chaos, spending five hours listening to meditation music through my headphones until I calmed my nervous system and stabilised my blood pressure. Yet, aside from my conversation with the Medical Superintendent, I found little meaningful support in the ward.

The staff felt distant, both figuratively and literally. I spent days observing the nurses, noticing a pattern that was hard to ignore. Two nurses rarely left their posts behind the glass doors, seemingly content to remain separated from the people they were meant to care for. Another nurse, supposed to oversee my care, spent most of his shift glued to his phone, repeatedly insisting he wasn't on social media despite what I'd witnessed. The lack of engagement wasn't just disheartening; it was alienating. They told me there wasn't enough work, but their inaction spoke volumes.

This detachment eroded the trust I might have otherwise placed in them. Trust, I've come to learn, is the cornerstone of recovery. Without it, even the best facilities can feel isolating. Driven by this realisation, I decided to take matters into my own hands. I approached the situation clearly and understood my rights and responsibilities, particularly under the Freedom of Information Act.

I explained to several nurses that keeping transparent, accurate, and collaborative notes wasn't just a bureaucratic requirement but essential for creating a therapeutic alliance. I then requested they print the Australian Quality and Safeguards Commission's Partners with Consumers standard to reinforce that care should never feel like an "Us vs. Them" dynamic. True collaboration, I argued, was vital to healing, not just for me but for anyone navigating the mental health system.

My advocacy, however, was not well-received. Some staff viewed my actions as challenging their authority rather than an effort to foster mutual respect. A visibly agitated nurse called me an "arrogant pig," clinging to his twenty years of experience as justification for dismissing my concerns. Another warden, perhaps less defensive but equally dismissive, bluntly told me, "I am not your partner."

That statement struck a nerve. His words encapsulated a mindset that perpetuates division rather than unity, that keeps patients as passive recipients of care instead of active participants in their recovery. In response, I decided to use humour as my shield and sword. Whenever he passed, I would salute him and cheerfully say, "Howdy, partner." At first, he ignored me, but eventually, my persistence wore him down. Unable to tolerate my antics, he arranged for my transfer to another ward.

The transfer was bittersweet. On one hand, it was a relief to leave an environment where collaboration felt like a foreign concept. On the other, it was a reminder of how far the mental health system still has to go. My experience in the ward wasn't just about inadequate care, it was a microcosm of a larger issue.

Healing cannot flourish in an adversarial environment. Caregivers and patients must walk the path of recovery together, not as opponents but as equals. My time in the High Dependency Unit reinforced this truth, even as it highlighted the systemic barriers that hinder its realisation.

True partnership in care is not just a lofty ideal; it's a necessity. And while I might not have won over every nurse or warden, I left that ward with my dignity intact and my voice stronger than ever, a small victory in the ongoing fight for compassionate, collaborative care.

Roll Call

My transition to the acute ward was like stepping into a new world. I was escorted to my room, a private, comfortable space equipped with a single bed, cupboards, an ensuite bathroom, and, most notably, a lock on the door. This small feature, absent in the High Dependency Unit, brought a sense of safety and control I hadn't felt in weeks.

The ward itself had a lighter, more social atmosphere. It reminded me of a backpacker's hostel, lively, full of conversations, and brimming with an undercurrent of possibility. I first come across Black Magic and his cousin, an Aboriginal man who radiated pride and wisdom as he shared stories of culture and history. They chatted with a young woman, excitedly anticipating the new chapter awaiting her after discharge the following day.

The energy around me felt hopeful for the first time in a while. The air buzzed with laughter and camaraderie, a stark contrast to the sterility of the High Dependency Unit. Yet, as inviting as it all seemed, I decided to observe quietly and rest. After a long, peaceful sleep, I woke feeling refreshed and inspired to document my impressions of the people I met, a roll call of the fascinating individuals who made the ward think like a community.

The Roll Call

- **Black Magic:** Now a trusted presence, he carried a quiet strength. Free from the chains of addiction, he reconnected with his country, finding healing and belonging in its vastness.
- **The Aboriginal Educator & Historian:** A charismatic storyteller, he taught me much about his heritage. A Jehovah's Witness yearning to reconnect with his ancestors, he dreamed of walking with elders. I promised to join him one day on this sacred journey.

- **ECT:** A survivor of homelessness, she battled a chemical imbalance that disrupted her life. Her resilience shone through, and I hoped for balance to return to her future.
- **Mood Disorder:** Struggling to grasp the fleeting nature of moods, she transformed as she embraced the idea that feelings were states, not permanent fixtures. Her newfound faith uplifted her.
- **The Botanist:** A genius passionate about solving the planet's biggest problems, from climate change to untapped dimensions of existence. Yet, even with all his knowledge, his learning journey had just begun.
- **Deafness:** Determined, yet resistant to learning, to his body and the doctors. His stubbornness blocked progress, but his potential remained undeniable.
- **Illiteracy:** Isolated by his struggles, he thrived once help reached him. Freed from boredom, he began to open up and connect with others.
- **Schizophrenia and Borderline:** Both lived in a world of delusions, making it difficult to bridge the gap of understanding. Yet, their presence served as a reminder of the complexities of mental health.
- **Angel:** A whirlwind of chaos and need, she spoke in her language and took without asking. But when met with compassion and patience, her joy became infectious.
- **The Complaints Mechanism:** Always grumbling, yearning for something to fix, but reluctant to act. She dreamed of returning to work, where her sense of purpose awaited.
- **Misery:** A quiet figure who kept to herself, embodying the shadows of the ward. I struggled to connect with her, but I respected her solitude.
- **Buddha:** On a journey of spiritual discovery, he sought wisdom in his traditions and carved out his unique path.

- **Generosity:** The heart of the ward. Wise beyond his years, he shared kindness, laughter, and wisdom, lifting the spirits of everyone around him.
- **The Prophet:** Lost in his phone, disconnected from the present, pacing endlessly. His potential seemed trapped behind the screen, and he stared blankly.
- **Jag:** Content with the comforts of TV, he missed the life happening around him, a reminder of the ease with which distractions consume us.
- **Gout:** Confined to a wheelchair, he struggled with lifestyle-related challenges. Yet, with hope and determination, he found the strength to walk again.
- **Pretty Boy:** Confident and vibrant, he embraced exercise and social connection, preparing eagerly to return to life outside.
- **The Wise Young Man:** A quiet force of wisdom, he disliked the food but helped clean up everyone's mess. When he spoke, we all listened, though his slow speech often tested our patience.
- **The Guardian Angel:** Once my helper in years past, her delusions now ran deep. She found joy in music and dance but struggled to navigate a world she no longer understood.
- **My Doppelgänger:** A mirror of myself, she carried both frustration and kindness. We bonded over shared experiences; her hugs and humour left a lasting impression.

As varied as the patients, the nurses brought their mix of energy. Some were exceptional partners in care, diving into traumas with empathy and offering a guiding hand. But most were distant, hiding behind glass doors, their demeanour marked by frustration and inflexibility. A few smiled, but many seemed weighed down by the "us vs. them" culture that hung heavy in the air.

Healing, I've come to realise, depends on partnership. True care is a collaboration, a meeting of equals where humanity is shared, not divided. In this ward, amidst its flaws and triumphs, I saw glimpses of what that could look like.

Jacky's Spirit

As soon as I transferred to the acute ward, I gravitated towards the Aboriginal Educator and Historian, Black Magic's cousin. His presence was magnetic, rooted in a profound pride for his Gundungurra, Darug, and Kamilaroi heritage. He carried a profound passion for educating others about Aboriginal culture, traditions, and history, offering me a glimpse into a world that had shaped him so completely.

The Educator was more than just a historian. He was a creator, running a clothing label called Pride in My Tribe Clothing Designs, a business showcasing Aboriginal artistry and culture through vibrant designs shared on Facebook. His energy seemed boundless, extending to organising events like the Jacky Brooks Cup, a spirited NAIDOC Week gala where teachers faced off against students in Oz Tag. He also championed the Jacky Brooks Medal, awarded to leading Aboriginal athletes—names like Greg Inglis and Patty Mills gracing its legacy.

He spoke with reverence about Jacky Brooks Track, nestled at Catalina Raceway in Katoomba—his mother's birthplace and a place that pulsed with ancestral significance. It was more than a physical space; it was a touchstone of identity, memory, and spirit. He was impatient to share this sacred site with me, his excitement sparking an idea that would soon evolve into something extraordinary.

As we talked, the seeds of a project began to take shape. We envisioned an adventure—a video capturing the essence of Aboriginal culture, history, and connection to the land. The plan was ambitious: a journey that would weave together stories from prominent Aboriginal elders, set against the backdrop of culturally significant locations.

We imagined beginning at La Perouse (Lapa), then moving to Parramatta (George Street), St Marys, Yarramundi, and

Katoomba. Each place had its unique story and connection to its people. St Marys was a pivotal site where the crossing of the Blue Mountains began at James Blaxland's farm. Brooks Lane Avenue in Agnes Banks was another cornerstone, a site that carried profound meaning for him and his ancestors. Katoomba held the Seven Sisters, a sacred narrative overshadowed by the Western tourist interpretation of the Three Sisters.

The Educator spoke passionately about including notable Aboriginal figures—football players like Mitchell Moses, Jerome Luai, Brian To'o, Stephen Crichton, and Josh Addo-Carr, as well as community leaders such as Aunt Carol Cooper and Aboriginal leader Bubble. He imagined involving Jim Angel, the longest-serving mayor of the Blue Mountains, and the Carlon family from the Megalong Valley. We decided to call the video *Jacky's Spirit*, a tribute to his grandmother and the enduring legacy of his family.

The more we talked, the more my excitement grew. Contributing to a project that honoured and amplified Aboriginal voices felt like a rare and profound privilege. His enthusiasm was infectious, inspiring me to reflect on my role in this cultural exchange.

Though he explained that I could not perform an Acknowledgment of Country due to my non-Indigenous heritage, he suggested that it might be possible for me to share a Welcome to Country. I thought carefully about this gesture of respect and composed the following:

"I would like to recognise the Traditional Custodians of the land on which we gather today, the Gundungurra people of the Darug nation. We recognise their continuing connection to the land, waters, and community and thank them for protecting the coastline since immemorial. The Traditional Owners of the land have maintained this country's delicate ecosystem for over 40,000 years. We pay respect to elders past and present and extend that respect to all First Nations people joining us here today. We can restore balance and bring about a unified nation by honouring the 100+ Aboriginal nations, their languages, and dialects."

Crafting those words felt like stepping onto sacred ground—an acknowledgment of the intricate relationship between people, land, and culture that had endured for millennia.

The Aboriginal Educator and Historian had shown me more than a history lesson. He had given me a window into the enduring spirit of his people, a reminder of the power of connection, and a spark of inspiration to carry forward in my journey. Together, we dreamed of creating something that would honour his ancestors, uplift his community, and share the profound beauty of Aboriginal culture with the world.

Surrendering to a Higher Power

In the stillness of my hospital days, I found myself reflecting deeply on all I had learned—not only during my time there but also in the weeks leading up to my arrival. These moments of introspection became a space where the concept of a Higher Power grew clearer, more expansive, and profoundly personal.

In her infinite wisdom, the Goddess had opened my mind to the idea that the term Higher Power transcends traditional definitions of "God." This broader interpretation resonated with the principles of balance and harmony I had encountered in Chinese Medicine, where the unseen forces of nature govern both the physical and spiritual realms.

I learned that surrendering to a higher power is not about relinquishing control or abandoning reason. It is about trust—a faith that there is an underlying harmony and intelligence guiding all things. It is the recognition that our paths are interwoven with the greater fabric of the universe, each thread contributing to a larger, incomprehensible whole.

Through surrender, I began to see the connections between all things—people, nature, spirit, and the cosmos. It was a shift from resistance to flow, fear to trust, and limitation to possibility. The Goddess had shown me that surrender is not the end of agency but the beginning of true alignment.

As I reflected, I realised that surrendering to a Higher Power was not an act of submission but one of empowerment. It allowed me to enter my place within the grand dance of existence, fully present and aware. In this surrender, I found peace and a profound sense of purpose—a purpose that resonated with the wisdom of the ages and the infinite possibilities of what is yet to come.

Wellness Revolution

As my understanding of surrender deepened, I began to see how it applied to my spiritual journey and the tangible world around me. During this time of reflection, the idea for a business, the Wellness Revolution, began to take shape—a vision inspired by the interplay of physical, mental, and spiritual health.

Over the past six months, I had envisioned a platform that would transform how people approached their well-being. Rooted in the principles of balance and alignment I had been exploring, the Wellness Revolution was more than just a business—it was a movement. It was a call to reimagine wellness not as a destination but as an ongoing co-creation process with one's Higher Power, community, and the larger forces of the universe.

Initially, I felt guided by the Goddess to create a Facebook page as a first step in sharing this vision. The page became a space where my ideas could evolve, and I dreamed of expanding it into something greater. At one point, I imagined launching the platform under the name *Messiah*, believing it could symbolise a universal solution to humanity's challenges, a digital manifestation of the salvation so many seek.

The morning after conceiving this idea, I woke with enthusiasm, ready to refine and implement it. But the Goddess, in her wisdom, swiftly dismantled the notion. "I will have nothing to do with a platform called Messiah," she said, highlighting its religious connotations and the risk of positioning the business as a divine entity. At first, I was disappointed, but as I reflected, I understood her guidance. The Wellness Revolution was not meant to emulate salvation as defined by any singular faith; rather, it was a vehicle for personal transformation and collective healing, open to all paths and possibilities.

I returned to the original name, Wellness Revolution, with renewed clarity and continued developing the concept. Inspired by the intersection of ancient wisdom and cutting-edge science, I composed a pitch to articulate my vision and set the stage for its realisation:

"The Wellness Revolution is a transformative course that will revolutionise how you approach wellness. By integrating diverse methodologies, Reiki, Traditional Chinese Medicine, Public Health, Measurement-Based Care, Precision Medicine, and more—this 16-week journey will reshape your understanding of yourself, your world, and your connection to a Higher Power. This program is designed to:

- Enhance your health and reduce physical and emotional burdens.
- Build resilience and cultivate a wise, balanced mind.
- Provide objective measurements of progress through health metrics.

Local wellness practitioners will guide participants through in-class exercises and at-home activities, fostering balance in the body, mental peace, and spiritual transformation. Participants will begin by signing the Higher Power Smart Contract, acknowledging their commitment to this revolutionary process. They will complete a demographic questionnaire, record an introductory video, and establish a baseline of their anthropometric, biochemical, and genomic profiles, creating a foundation for measurable progress."

Upon enrolment, participants will receive a personalised participation pack, including a gift from Us 'N' U—a symbol of unity and support as they embark on this transformative journey.

The Wellness Revolution is not merely a course; it is a community, a commitment, and a calling to align with the highest version of yourself.
If you are ready to experience a profound transformation, you are among the luckiest 20 people on the planet to join the inaugural cohort of the Wellness Revolution.

As I wrote the pitch, I felt a surge of energy, as though the idea had a life of its own. It was more than a business proposal; it was an offering, a bridge connecting the wisdom of ancient traditions with the promise of modern innovation.

I reached out to a friend, a talented videographer, to discuss creating a promotional video for the platform. I envisioned this video as a powerful introduction to the Wellness Revolution, capturing its essence and inviting others to join.

Through this process, I realised the Wellness Revolution reflected my journey, a call to align body, mind, and spirit and embrace the possibilities that emerge when we surrender to a Higher Power. This surrender was not about relinquishing control but trusting in guidance from within and beyond.

At its core, the Wellness Revolution was an invitation to co-create a new way of living that acknowledges the interconnectedness of all things and the transformative power of aligning with the universal flow.

As I moved forward with the project, I felt a deep sense of purpose, knowing that the Wellness Revolution could spark meaningful change for its participants and the world.

Investment

While the concept of the Wellness Revolution was evolving into something extraordinary, I began contemplating the broader idea of investment. I wanted to create a world where everyone could share in the prosperity of a global initiative. The name "Messiah" had already been discarded after upsetting the Goddess, so my friend and I explored alternatives. We landed on "Us 'N' U", an inclusive and inspiring name. Shortly after leaving the hospital, I registered it as a business name, feeling that it embodied the essence of unity and collaboration.

The Wellness Revolution was a solid foundation, but I realised that to expand its reach, I needed investors. Not just traditional investors, but a system where everyone, regardless of financial status, could participate. This idea sparked a new pitch, one that I believed could revolutionise the world:

"Why do you invest? Is it for yourself? For your family? For your company, nation, or humanity? Is it for the planet's wellbeing or to support a cause close to your heart? Whatever your reasons, you invest because you care about creating a better future. At Us 'N' U, we share this vision."

"We are not just another company seeking investments. We are an organisation redefining what investing means. For as little as $1, anyone can become an equal shareholder in Us 'N' U. Yes, equal. By investing, you join a global community of like-minded individuals dedicated to solving the world's greatest challenges. Together, we raise funds, develop innovative solutions, and create a better future for all."

"Imagine this: every dollar invested is a vote for peace, prosperity, and progress. The funds we raise will go towards employing the brightest minds, developing transformative technologies, and addressing humanity's most pressing needs. And as a shareholder, you are not just contributing. You are part of a consensus-driven organisation where every decision requires 100 per cent agreement. No more power imbalances, no more exploitation. Just equality, transparency, and shared success."

"This is your chance to invest in a future where everyone thrives. With Us 'N' U, you are not just investing in a company. You are investing in humanity, our planet, and yourself. Sign our smart contract, secure your share, and watch your investment grow financially and in the impact it creates. Together, we can achieve the unimaginable."

At the time, I genuinely believed I had stumbled upon the solution to all the world's problems. The idea of equal investment, where even the poorest could afford to participate, seemed flawless. If everyone were equal partners in a global enterprise, we could pool resources, eliminate inequality, and create a system where everyone had a voice.

But as I reflected, cracks in my logic began to appear. How would such a system be implemented? Could everyone truly have an equal share of all the world's wealth and resources? Would it be possible to convince billions of people to participate? These were questions I had not yet answered.

Looking back, I see the beauty and naivety in my vision. The dream of universal equality and shared prosperity is noble. Still, it requires more than idealism; it demands careful planning, realistic frameworks, and the ability to navigate the complexities of human behaviour and global systems. While the pitch may not have been as flawless as I initially thought, it planted a seed, a vision of what could be possible if humanity worked together.

Guardian Angel

While on the ward, I met a woman who claimed to be a Guardian Angel. Her presence was calm and enigmatic, and her surreal story captivated my attention. She told me she had crossed my path during a difficult chapter of my life at Cumberland Hospital. She recounted a memory from years ago when her son had tried to comfort me during a moment of despair in Parramatta.

As she told it, her son had hugged me to soothe my distress. However, the police who witnessed the interaction chose not to see it as an act of kindness but rather as an opportunity for ridicule. She described how they mocked us with cruel slurs before arresting us both. According to her, we were taken to Cumberland Hospital, where we were confined in chambers for 15 days without food or water. She claimed it was only after she contacted a lawyer and threatened the hospital wardens that they finally released us.

Her story was shocking, and I found myself questioning its accuracy. Yet the conviction in her voice and the detail in her recollection gave me pause. Whether or not her version of events was entirely true, it seemed rooted in her belief that she had been sent to protect me.

She told me she had been watching over me ever since that time, praying for me regularly. As we spoke, she offered to "bless" me, placing her hands gently on me as she declared her angelic nature. "You couldn't see it back then," she said, "but I am an angel. If you open your mind to the possibility of angels, you will perceive us one day."

Her words were both strange and comforting. Her voice showed undeniable sincerity, as if she truly believed in her celestial mission. She explained that she always knew we would meet again and had been watching me, ensuring that I remained safe even through my darkest times.

Reflecting on our conversation, I was caught between scepticism and wonder. Was she truly a Guardian Angel, or was her identity a product of her struggles? Either way, the experience left me pondering the unseen forces in life, the people, energies, and perhaps even divine beings that may guide and protect us, whether we realise it or not.

Experiences Through Trial and Error

One afternoon, I spotted the Botanist scribbling furiously on the whiteboard, his mind engrossed in a maze of equations. Intrigued by his intensity, I set aside what I was doing and wandered closer. Before long, a small group of us had gathered, captivated by the Botanist's passionate explanations.

The Botanist was a fascinating character. He was a short man with a full beard and an aura of unrestrained curiosity. Just the day before, he had shared his dream of starting a heavy metal band and his thoughts on music's profound impact on human consciousness. He spoke enthusiastically about Sun Ra's cosmic jazz and how music not only influences listeners but also shapes the minds of musicians.

Now, standing before the whiteboard, he turned our attention to chemical structures, dopamine, serotonin, and essential amino acids. With each stroke of the marker, he illustrated how minor changes in chemical bonds could drastically alter the behaviour of entire systems. His explanations blended scientific precision with shamanic wonder, inviting us into his world.

The Botanist shared stories that walked the line between science and mythology. He spoke of his experiments with the chemical structure of LSD to create compounds that profoundly affected the body and mind. In one particularly wild tale, he described crafting an analgesic so potent that it allowed him to endure a severe beating from the police without feeling pain. We were equal parts horrified and awestruck.

He also sketched out an electrolysis machine capable of converting hydrogen into water and vice versa, a vision he described as part of a larger ambition to harness the elemental forces of nature. His ideas flowed like an endless river, each concept feeding into the next.

That night, the Botanist barely slept. Driven by an insatiable hunger for discovery, he filled an entire notebook with equations and sketches. He pored over books on plant medicines, meticulously studying *The Encyclopedia of Psychoactive Plants* and citing the works of Rick Doblin, the Multidisciplinary Association for Psychedelic Studies (MAPS), and spiritual thinkers like Sadhguru.

He described himself as a shaman and a psychonaut, a seeker who learns through "trial and error." His methods were unconventional, blending rigorous scientific exploration with an intuitive understanding of the mind and its connection to nature. Beyond the chemical compounds and psychoactive substances, the Botanist shared insights into alternative ways to expand consciousness without drugs. His ideas were revolutionary and deeply thought-provoking.

Listening to the Botanist felt like embarking on a journey through the intersections of science, spirituality, and creativity. It was a world where chemistry became a tool for understanding the material universe and probing the depths of human experience. For those lucky enough to hear him speak, it was an unforgettable exploration of possibility.

Experts by Experience

I introduced myself to a nurse I hadn't yet met. She told me she was new to the service and had been appointed as the Nursing Educator. Her role was to train the staff on Early Psychosis, and she invited a few members of the peer workforce to speak alongside the Headspace team, who were scheduled to present on the topic.

At first, this news excited me. Here was a chance to share firsthand insight into how Early Psychosis had affected my life and how valuable such a program would have been for me during my younger years. I had studied Early Psychosis programs globally and even mapped out various frameworks through my research. I knew the International Early Psychosis Association (IEPA) and its Melbourne-based database. I shared this with the nurse, expressing how my lived experience could provide a unique perspective that would enrich staff training. I saw myself not just as a patient but as an "expert by experience," someone who had not only survived but actively engaged with the mental health system, advocating for change from within.

I was certain that this opportunity could offer a new, nuanced layer to the training, something no textbook could offer, a real, unvarnished account of the lived reality of psychosis. I believed this would resonate more deeply with staff than the theoretical knowledge they were likely being taught. My experience, both as someone who had endured the isolation, confusion, and stigma of Early Psychosis and as a mentor to those navigating similar paths, had equipped me with invaluable insights.

However, my excitement was short-lived. I was reminded that I was still in an inpatient unit, a space where patients' voices, no matter how qualified, often seemed to be dismissed. I was told that if I wanted to contribute to the Early Psychosis Program, I would have to apply for a position when one became available. The message was clear: my lived experience wasn't enough to warrant immediate inclusion in the program, no matter how rich or relevant. I was left to walk away from the conversation, frustrated and disillusioned.

At that moment, the gap between theoretical and lived expertise was laid bare. Despite my research, international presentations, and direct experience, my perspective seemed undervalued in favour of academic qualifications. In my mind, this dismissal wasn't just frustrating, it was a systemic failure.

It struck me that mental health professionals, while highly trained, often have limited understanding of the emotional and psychological turmoil someone experiences in the throes of psychosis. No matter how many textbooks they read, they could never fully grasp the experience unless they had lived through it themselves. It's this truth that people with lived experience, like me, can provide, a perspective that challenges the conventional framework and offers deep insights into how the system could be improved.

Lived experience holds a form of wisdom that professional training cannot replicate. In my years of interacting with clinicians, mentoring young leaders, and presenting to international audiences, I have come to believe that those who have survived psychosis bring a level of insight that theory alone can never offer.

What clinicians often lack is a visceral understanding of what it is like to be at the mercy of a broken system, to struggle with the terror of losing touch with reality, and to navigate the labyrinth of mental health care. The practical wisdom embedded in lived experience and the ability to articulate the personal, emotional, and spiritual struggles encountered along the way offers a powerful tool for training those who serve in the mental health field.

A question-and-answer session with someone who has survived psychosis would be a rare, invaluable learning opportunity for professionals. It would challenge their assumptions, expand their understanding, and help them see beyond the clinical and into the human experience. Yet, once again, the system disregarded the expertise it was so eager to call upon when needed most.

It became painfully clear that in a system dominated by clinical and academic gatekeeping, those with the most to offer, the "experts by experience," are often silenced or sidelined. This isn't just a missed opportunity. It is a systemic failure to acknowledge the true depth of expertise that exists beyond the confines of professional credentials. As I walked away from that encounter, I couldn't help but think this is why the system is so broken. It thrives on the belief that textbooks and credentials can replace lived wisdom when, in reality, the two must work in concert to create a truly compassionate, effective mental health system.

Andrew Turtle

Happenings at the Nut Home

The Hungry Man wasn't eating. Instead, he drowned his hunger with long necks of beer, which only seemed to fuel his anger. But with a single point of pressure and a healing intention, the anger vanished, if only he could believe it. In that moment, he met Generosity and was nourished. He decided to feast on Generosity for the rest of his life, and after that, hunger was no longer his companion.

Once trapped in her despair, Misery realised her power and began dancing with the Great Storyteller. Witnessing her smile and laughter echoing in the room was a beautiful sight. When she allowed herself to smile, her face came alive, and she became stunningly beautiful.

Mood Disorder wasn't yet ready to release her anger and fully embrace the story. Her state of mind clung to the pain, preventing her from finding the happiness she deserved.

The Wise Young Man paced restlessly, holding onto his food, unwilling to share it. He recognised Generosity but couldn't yet open his heart to it. He was wise beyond his years but not generous enough yet.

Monty Python, full of wit and joy, remained misunderstood by others. People weren't yet humorous enough to appreciate his satire. If only they could see the humour in their own stories, they might find fewer thorns on their side. Every time I spoke with Monty Python, he made me laugh, a reminder of the healing power of levity.

Pretty Boy kept his body looking perfect but wore headphones to block out the noise of the world around him. He longed to escape, party, and find meaning in something other than his reflection.

Mood Disorder, riding a bike, looked miserable, her face a picture of frustration. But when she smiled, it was as though the pedals moved faster, as though she could finally start to believe in her beauty. That smile, radiant and full of light, could change everything.

The Greatest Storyteller shook Pretty Boy to his core. He didn't realise he didn't need to numb himself with ice or distractions because the party was already here, within him. He just had to open his eyes and let it in.

Illiteracy and the Wise Young Man sat together, sharing information on their phones. But neither was ready to accept the gifts Generosity had given them. They still thought the things they had were theirs alone, not realising that happiness comes from sharing, not owning.

Angel sat miserably despite everyone else's generosity. She was not yet ready to give, only to take, and this continued to weigh her down. If only she could understand that she already had everything she needed.

Deafness, unable to truly hear, began to listen to Generosity. His eyes lit up, his face showing the first signs of joy. He still spoke of Illiteracy, but the warmth of Generosity was slowly reaching him. The Great Storyteller didn't mind that only Generosity seemed to appreciate the tale; he knew it was already a masterpiece in his mind. Generosity gave so much and, in return, received so much more. He wanted everything, and by giving everything, he had everything.

Anger continued to rage, ignoring everyone and everything. He craved control, but his attempts only fuelled his fury. If only he had realised that letting go of control could ease his anger instead of letting it control him.

ECT still doubted whether the treatment was working. She had yet to realise that happiness doesn't come from a molecule, a neurotransmitter, or even a neuron. No, happiness won't come with ECT until she learns to find joy within herself and embrace joy from within.

Illiteracy was coming to life. He was doing everything he could to break free from this place, slowly warming to Generosity and growing stronger each day.

Pretty Boy, wrongfully imprisoned for a crime he didn't commit, found himself isolated. His only crime? Being too goddamn good-looking. No one seemed willing to help him, and he couldn't understand why. Jealousy must have been at play. Could they not see his beauty?

Illiteracy now savoured his food, no longer taking it for granted. Gratefulness was transforming him, and with each meal, he grew stronger. I hope he reads the story one day to understand how much the Great Storyteller respects him.

The Invisible One remained hidden in her room, unnoticed by most. If only they would open their eyes, they could see her too.

The Prophet passed by the Great Storyteller, issuing a vague warning. Was it a threat, or just a proclamation? He laid down the law, but the true danger of lawgiving lies in letting it dominate one's thoughts without understanding.

Illiteracy was gaining power. Now, with voice-to-text technology at his fingertips, he was unstoppable. No one could mess with him now that Generosity was on his side. He dreamed of dictating for the nation.

Generosity, the Hungry Man, and Monty Python gathered for a good laugh, playing a round of Jumanji. None of them wanted to die. They were too alive at this moment.

The Man entered the story, but just as quickly, he was gone. Where did the Mango go? Was he ever really here at all?

The Wise Young Man smiled, talking to Generosity, beginning to believe in his power. When he smiled, I couldn't help but love it. The Wise Young Man could turn Heaven into Hell and Hell into Heaven.

The Great Marine Biologist took us back to childhood, recounting stories of sharks. Then, speaking with Generosity, I realised how essential the ocean was to the story, how salt is to saltwater. The Great Goddess Earth needs salt water to restore her balance.

Intimidation craved power, taking what she did not possess. She raised her voice, threatened me, and even forced Generosity to take medication against his will.

The lawgiver remained silent, and I misunderstood. But I now see him as the lore-giver. I am ready to listen to his story when he is prepared to share it.

ECT sat down, trying to solve the maze of her thoughts. She feared returning home, knowing that fear awaited her. If only she had realised that she was already home, that peace could have been found wherever she was. I want her to know I believe in her and hope she finds that peace.

The Prophet was frustrated, shouting at everyone because no one would listen. He had yet to realise that for others to hear him, he had first to speak openly, to share what was going on in his mind. It's impossible to help others if you're unwilling to help yourself.

Angel, the thief, was now drawing on the walls, a thief and a graffiti artist. Her vibrant and beautiful drawings brought colour to this otherwise dark place

Andrew Turtle

Where Are You?

Intimidation gave Generosity medication against his will, so I confronted her. I asked why she chose to take away Generosity's power. Her response was simple: "He needed it."

I told her that it was a violation of human rights, a form of substituted decision-making.

She asked, "Where are we?"

I replied, "We are here on Earth, and human rights should never be taken from anyone."

She repeated the question, "Where are we?"

And I said, "The same place as you."

It seemed incomprehensible to me. Just because we are in a mental health hospital, it shouldn't mean our human rights are any less valid than anywhere else. We are human beings. It shouldn't matter where I am.

She walked away.

As I stood there, I thought, I know exactly where I am. I have to ask someone for soap, laundry detergent, and shampoo. I need someone to help me open the door.

Intimidation can go to the shop on her way home from work and get whatever she needs, no questions asked. She can return to her partner, receive a hug, and sleep in her home. I've seen my girlfriend for only two hours in the last three weeks. When COVID hit, I wasn't allowed visitors.

I realised I couldn't even go for a walk outside the courtyard. I had not seen a tree in almost three weeks nor experienced the simple luxury of stepping outside the hospital walls for a breath of fresh air. And still, Intimidation reminds me where I am. Yes, I know exactly where I am.

I am in a place where the gym is closed, the massage chair is broken, my phone is hacked, and my headphones cannot be used because they rely on my phone. I wait for others to contact me. I pace through a lonely corridor, tired of walking up and down the same walls. I am weary of having nothing to do. This place has broken me. What is my treatment plan? What is my wellness plan? Yes, I know where I am.

The next day, every time I approached Intimidation, I asked, "Where are you?"

By the end of the day, I was pulled aside for repeating the words prescribed to me just a day earlier. Yes, I went too far. However, I believed it was acceptable for staff to intimidate patients. When those same words are mirrored back, the patient is suddenly the bully.

I had reached my limit. I had been ignored so many times. I had been given no support. Now, I felt intimidated by someone who was supposed to care for me, someone who was meant to look out for me, not control me.

And in that moment, I finally understood where I was.

I was in a place where my rights were continually disregarded, where my needs were ignored, and where the very people who should have been supporting me were contributing to my sense of powerlessness.

But now, I knew where I was. And I had had enough.

Gout Lost It

Gout lost it! I wouldn't call it "aggression," but he expressed big emotions. He was fed up, fed up with being touched inappropriately, even by the nurses. Intimidation had spoken to him as though he wasn't human, and on top of that, people kept touching him without respect for his boundaries.

He was expressing his feelings, and sometimes you must yell when you're pushed to your limit. His outburst wasn't just anger; it was a cry for recognition, a plea for someone to see him as a person, not a problem.

I hope that, in time, Gout receives the care he needs, care that listens, truly listens, and validates his experiences, because that's all anyone needs, to be heard.

2 Hours Each Day

I asked a manager why the nurses seemed so reluctant to help. I pointed out that the nurses work eight-hour shifts and are responsible for five patients each. If a nurse spent just twenty minutes with each patient as a baseline, that would be two hours of their shift, leaving them six hours to complete the necessary paperwork.

Those twenty minutes could be used for a simple check-in, a moment to understand how each person is feeling, talk about their story, unpack their trauma, and review their notes. It would allow us to share more of who we are and for them to get to know us better.

This shift in approach could transform the dynamic from an "Us vs. Them" mentality to something far more meaningful, a therapeutic relationship built on mutual respect and understanding. Nurses could share their expertise in ways that empower patients to become more informed and capable decision-makers.

Rather than making substituted decisions for us, this new approach would create a space where we, as patients, could feel supported in making our own choices. It is not just about being able to make decisions when unwell but about laying the foundation for our lives in the community. This is about building a true partnership where both parties feel heard and valued and where the focus is not on control but healing.

Healing together.

Scribblings & Visits in the Hospital

While in the hospital, I immersed myself in reading and writing. Writing became both an outlet and a way to process the experiences of those around me. I wrote about the people, the interactions, and the musings within the ward, much of what you are reading now. I also turned to the Bible, working through a 40-day study guide in the massage chair room. As my attention allowed, I delved into portions of *DBT for Dummies*, which helped me better understand agreements and dialectics. In addition to these readings, I filled three scribbling books, reflecting on my work life and exploring areas of my existence that troubled me.

On the day I was brought to the hospital, I had been consumed with anger, particularly toward my mother, whom I blamed for getting me there. When I questioned my rights, I was introduced to the Carers Statement, which allowed me to choose who would be involved in my care. Still wrapped in anger, I didn't want my parents to be part of that process. I can't fully explain why I didn't ask the Goddess, my girlfriend, to be my next of kin. Instead, I turned to my ex-girlfriend, the Best Friend, and asked her to take that role. She visited me several times, providing much-needed companionship and an opportunity to share some of my writings.

The situation with the Goddess grew increasingly complicated due to the lack of contact. My parents, perhaps out of frustration or misunderstanding, told her I didn't want anything to do with her. This was not true, but I had no way to reach out to her at the time. Eventually, she contacted me and gave me her number, and we reconnected. When she drove down from Newcastle to visit, it was a much-needed reunion. The Goddess and I had a beautiful visit, sharing an hour, arm in arm, reconnecting and smoothing over the misunderstandings. From there, we stayed in touch regularly, exchanging life updates and supporting each other through challenges.

Although I had explicitly requested not to involve my parents in my care, there came a point when I called my mum. She had been battling depression, staying in bed for several days, weighed down by guilt over how I had treated her. She was deeply affected by the incident when I jumped out of the car, thinking she had run me over, and the subsequent decision to have me hospitalised. Despite her struggles, she made her way to see me.

My dad and mum arrived for a brief visit. The details of that conversation were hazy, but there was an undeniable tension between us. Things didn't go well, and my frustration and anger, fuelled by my time in the hospital, were likely palpable. My words, harsh as they were, reflected the turmoil inside. Eventually, my dad spoke the words that pierced it all: "It's just too hurtful."

Throughout the period leading up to and during my hospitalisation, I wasn't myself. Looking back at the scribblings, especially the ones I chose not to share, there was so much anger and frustration, much of it not entirely justifiable. I wasn't grounded in what was rational and what was not. I suppose this is the dialectic nature of mania, oscillating between extremes of emotion and struggling to find balance amidst chaos.

Treatment Plan

In an attempt to advocate for my healing, I wrote a letter to the psychiatrist, hoping to initiate a meaningful review of my treatment plan and, potentially, a change in diagnosis. I have been on medication for schizophrenia since I was fifteen, and throughout the years, I've faced intense delusions that have ebbed and flowed in their severity. However, I have reached a pivotal moment where I can finally say that I have moved beyond the God Delusion. I no longer see myself as Jesus Christ but recognise myself as the creator of my story, shaping my narrative and understanding.

While this clarity has been liberating, I believe it's time to reassess my diagnosis. Over the years, the affective aspects of my condition have grown more prominent. The highs and lows and the irrational mood swings have become more pronounced, particularly when faced with stress. I recognise now that these mood fluctuations, alongside the traumas I experienced as a teenager, led me to seek ways to "escape my reality". These delusions, which once seemed so consuming, now feel like they are part of a past I'm moving beyond. Still, the emotional aspect remains, which has increasingly become central to my experience.

Recent challenges, particularly struggles in my professional life, have exacerbated these emotional fluctuations, leading to job losses and a steady erosion of my confidence. It feels as though the mood component has become the dominant force in my life. I'm beginning to wonder whether schizoaffective disorder may better reflect my lived experience, one that requires medication addressing both the psychotic and the mood-related symptoms.

Sleep, too, has always been a challenge for me. Since I was fifteen, I have struggled with insomnia, and it continues to be an issue that demands attention and support.

I seek a safe and supportive environment to explore these complexities. I believe the Hills Clinic offers the best opportunity for me to heal. I've begun to touch on some of the traumas from my past, and I hope to work through these more deeply in group therapy. My goal is not only to resolve old wounds but also to develop strategies to navigate daily life with greater resilience. With the right guidance and support, I hope to continue my healing journey and build a foundation of self-awareness and strength.

I am asking you, as my psychiatrist, to advocate for me in this process. Your guidance is crucial in helping me find the path towards healing and growth. I hope we can craft a treatment plan that nurtures all aspects of my well-being, allowing me to move forward with clarity, stability, and the courage to live a more balanced life.

Hungry Man is Hungry

Hungry Man is hungry. It's not just that he's hungry in the conventional sense; he's battling an eating disorder that only allows him to keep down crackers and cheese. Anything else, and his body rejects it. The dietician had worked with him to create a specialised plan, ensuring he would only consume rice crackers, a manageable option for his fragile condition. A chart was even drawn up to reflect this carefully considered approach.

Yet, when Hungry Man arrived at the dinner table, the food he needed wasn't there. Generosity, seeing his distress, stood up for him, advocating for the care Hungry Man required. Unfortunately, that act of compassion led to trouble for Generosity.

A nurse came out, offering Hungry Man a sandwich. Knowing he couldn't eat it without throwing up, Hungry Man expressed his concern. "I'll throw it up," he said. But the nurse, seemingly dismissing his plea, responded curtly, "That's the only option we have."

When he repeated that he couldn't eat it, she reiterated, "That's all we have." The frustration was palpable as Hungry Man was forced into a corner. "But I will throw it up," he pleaded again, but his words were brushed aside. The nurse's irritation grew, and in the end, Hungry Man was left without food, his hunger unmet, and his condition worsening.

He went hungry. Once again, the Hungry Man found himself starving, not just physically but emotionally, as the system failed to meet his needs. In a place where care is supposed to be the priority, it felt like the hunger went unnoticed, and he was left to suffer even more.

The Guardian Angel's Delusions

The Guardian Angel shared various bizarre and vivid stories with me, each seeming more fantastical than the last. She spoke of her backyard, claiming to have an elephant, a rhinoceros, an orangutan, kangaroos, and wallabies. Among them, she insisted, was a peach, white, and red Kawasaki motorbike. She also told me she was pregnant with quadruplets, feeling them "kicking like hell", and just wanted to go home to be with her five dingoes. These dingoes, she said, were all from the same mother and father.

She spoke of her life and her family with great emotion. The Guardian Angel described her two German shepherds and how she longed to reunite with them. She also mentioned her brothers, her thirty-two children, and her husband. According to her, her husband worked for the Federal Police in Internal Affairs. However, she claimed that everything was corrupt, and he had the power to make things go away by arresting people under him.

In one of her more troubling revelations, the Guardian Angel spoke of her involvement in a corruption inquiry. She claimed that the NDIS should compensate her for the deaths of her two brothers. One, she said, was shot through the head; the other endured unimaginable injuries. She spoke of how the second brother's brain remained intact despite his injuries and how he had turned into an angel after his death.

"I'm an angel," she would say with a smile that seemed detached from the grimness of her words.

The stories continued, more surreal than before. She claimed that a dingo had injected ice, and then she licked my spoon, telling me that the dingo's drug addiction had been passed on to her. With unsettling conviction, the Guardian Angel said she had to give this dingo one hundred kilograms of something every day to keep it alive, even claiming the dingo had become a bomb squad dog with long nails, using them to handle explosives. She said the dingo had also had twenty-nine pups, though one had died, leaving twenty-eight in the litter.

Then she spoke of a man named Ridgy Didge, her partner, who she said was still alive.

Through all of her declarations, it was clear that the Guardian Angel was trapped in a maze of delusions. She spoke with such urgency and detail that it was impossible to ignore the intensity of her belief. In her mind, these narratives were real, her reality intertwined with vivid images of animals, family, and a world full of corruption, loss, and a desire to return home.

But the question remained: how much of this was the manifestation of her suffering, and how much was simply a mind grappling with its broken pieces?

Angel Goes Through My Clothes

I was in my room, desperately trying to rest and recharge, hoping to calm my anxiety. I needed sleep more than anything. But then Angel came in, rummaging through my clothes without regard for what I was going through. She asked if she could take some shorts. I didn't mind at first, as she explained that she had "pissed her pants and had no clothes to wear". I agreed, but then she asked if she could wear two pairs of shorts.

I couldn't understand why anyone would need two pairs of shorts.

Frustration overwhelmed me, and I snapped, "I need to sleep. You can have one pair of shorts. Don't you understand how I'm feeling? I need rest. Don't you understand emotions?"

She replied, "No."

That was enough. I got up and locked the door to avoid being disturbed.

The next morning, I woke up and immediately locked the door again before sitting down to write. Angel wasn't wearing my shorts, so I asked if I could have them back. She told me she had already returned them. I was confused. How could that be when I had locked the door?

With the help of the nurses, I opened the door. To my surprise, my shorts were sitting there. I wondered how Angel had gotten in, given that I had locked the door the night before and also locked it first thing in the morning before sitting down to write.

Moments like these made me feel insecure. Everything was unsettling, and I couldn't shake the feeling that something was off, yet I couldn't quite grasp what it was.

My Trigger

I took some time to reflect, digging deeper into my emotional responses, and I realised that my trigger was being spoken to in a raised tone. Though I understand that this isn't always done out of anger and can sometimes be a reflection of someone's passion, it often feels threatening to me. When the tone rises, it feels like a loss of control, and my sense of safety starts slipping away. In those moments, I tend to express "big emotions", which seem to take over and feel impossible to manage.

I know that a raised tone is sometimes a necessary expression to regain control in a situation. But for me, it often feels like an erosion of my power, and that's when my reactions spiral beyond my ability to hold them in check. The sense of being diminished, even unintentionally, triggers a response that feels like I am losing myself in that moment.

I don't want people to be angry anymore. I don't want them to raise their voices at me, not because I don't understand communication dynamics, but because I don't want to ignite my trigger. I want to stop the cycle of anger before it even begins. If I can avoid being triggered, then I won't respond with yelling. But I also know that it's not just about me. I also need to stop yelling at others so that I don't provoke their triggers. I understand that this dynamic flows both ways and requires a conscious effort to hold space for one another's emotional boundaries.

Gout Writes on the Board

Gout wrote the following questions on the whiteboard:

- Does the walker choose the path, or does the path choose the walker?
- Are the paths we see all there is?
- Or are there other paths we cannot see because we aren't in the right place to see them?

I paused, reflecting on the depth of his questions, and then responded. I told Gout that he wasn't asking the right questions, or rather, that his answers wouldn't lead to the right request. I gently reminded him that he was, in fact, in the right place to see, as he had already taught me how to see better. Yet I felt that he wasn't practising his wisdom.

I explained that all the answers were already there, within the vastness of his mind and the limits of his imagination. The pathways existed, but it was a matter of how deeply one could perceive and feel.

He countered, saying, "Perceive is a better word to describe what we see, but what we see isn't all we perceive."

I nodded and replied, "Perception is merely your brain's interpretation of what it has processed based on its received inputs. The body tracks and provides that feedback. So one of the most important questions you can ask yourself is, 'How do I feel?' But you're not yet ready to answer that question honestly. Otherwise, the walker would choose his path."

And just like that, Gout was gone, unwilling to let me answer his question. He wasn't yet ready to listen to his feelings or to open himself to the possibility of change. If he truly allowed himself to feel, he would see that he could walk, and that the wheelchair wouldn't need to define him. Instead, he clung to anger and self-pity, unable to accept the possibility that the power to transform was in his own hands.

Even though Gout had physically walked away from me, his anger, depression, and resistance remained. He wasn't ready to step into the journey of healing. He wasn't yet prepared to fully understand what he could perceive or become.

Dialectics

Generosity, and I found profound solace in discussing dialectics. We were deeply comforted by the realisation that we could reach an agreement simply by agreeing to disagree. Both sides of an argument could hold truth, and we could both be right.

I reflected on a passage from *DBT For Dummies* highlighting how disagreements are a natural part of human interaction. It emphasised that it's acceptable to disagree skilfully, but it's also important to recognise the wisdom in the other person's perspective and allow that to exist alongside our own. This is the practice of "agreeing to disagree". Alternatively, both parties can acknowledge the validity of the other's viewpoint, an outcome that arises when both remain curious and open, allowing for the integration of new insights. A third approach involves a synthesis, where a new perspective emerges, combining the strengths of both viewpoints. Throughout this process, the goal is to remain open to ideas we might have previously missed, thereby expanding our consciousness.

For Generosity and me, dialectics became a tool for resolving inner and outer conflicts. Generosity had encountered the concept years ago during his philosophy studies, and it resonated deeply with him as a path for harmonious resolution. Whether finding an answer over breakfast or navigating a deeper conversation later in the day, dialectics offered clarity.

It became clear that disagreeing was not only permissible but also empowering. Every person's perspective, shaped by their experiences and emotions, is their best perspective at any given moment. If a perspective feels right for someone, it is right for them. In that recognition, a deeper peace arises. For Generosity and me, dialectics illuminated the path to understanding. By embracing the validity of each person's point of view, we could transcend conflict and find connection.

In our discussions, we realised that dialectics wasn't just a philosophical concept but a tool for spiritual growth. It invited us to expand our capacity to see through others' eyes, meet them where they were, and honour the truths they held, even if they differed from ours. It was a practice that transcended argument and ventured into the realm of unity, inviting us to recognise that the path to peace is often found in the willingness to hold space for differing perspectives, all contributing to the vastness of human experience.

A Football

It's incredible how something as simple as a football can shift the atmosphere in a mental health hospital. A football, an unassuming object, can uplift spirits and bring people together when the mind feels overwhelmed by the absence of activity and engagement. Football became a bridge to joy in a place where the days can feel long and aimless. It was just a ball, yet it invited laughter, creativity, and connection, with each person contributing their unique skills and playing their own game.

With his characteristic flair, Generosity kicked the ball AFL-style, proud of his recent award for most improved. "Thank you for coming along," he joked as he lined up his next move. First, he tried handballing the ball, but the shape wasn't quite right. It wasn't leather and didn't bounce as he expected, but it didn't matter. He was free in the moment, not bound by the rules or the shape of the game.

He then attempted to teach Monty Python how to bounce the ball, which proved difficult too. It wasn't the right type of ball for the bounce he was used to. But the fun was in the effort, in the attempt to connect, share, and laugh together. The ball didn't need to be perfect; it only needed to be present, and that presence created space for joy.

The Man, whom I assumed would gravitate towards boxing, surprised us all by taking on the quarterback role. His passes were spot on, guiding us to imaginary touchdowns with ease. At one point, when he didn't want to handball, he performed a header instead. Soccer had been part of his past, and the familiar motion sparked a memory, connecting him to a sense of mastery.

At that moment, the game wasn't about the rules. It was about being present, being in the moment, and allowing ourselves to play. We passed the ball like rugby league stars, and the air around us seemed to hum with possibility.

It didn't matter what game we played. For the first time in what felt like forever, I was laughing. I was happy. I had something to do, something to focus on. I was reminded of the simple joys found in movement and connection. Sport, for me, was a portal to creativity. I loved being in my imagination, where the boundaries of possibility dissolved and everything became attainable.

At that moment, I realised joy could be found in the most unexpected places. A football was more than just a ball; it was a tool for connection, healing, and remembering that even in the most challenging times, we can find reasons to smile, engage, and share in the lightness of being.

Dungeons and Dragons

Gout's face lit up with excitement as he shared his passion for Dungeons and Dragons (D&D) with Monty Python. He had been running D&D groups for years, immersing himself in the intricate world of fantasy, storytelling, and strategic play. Now, as if offering a piece of his soul, he proudly presented his most treasured possessions: rare dice, maps, and meticulously crafted character sheets. Yet, despite his openness, there was one boundary he wasn't ready to cross; he wouldn't let me touch them. They held too much monetary and sentimental value, and even the smallest fingerprint felt like a risk he couldn't afford. His reluctance wasn't just about physical preservation; it was a reflection of the emotional walls he had built to protect his passions and his heart.

I understood, though. I saw his enthusiasm and love for the game, and how it allowed him to explore new worlds and deeper parts of himself. He might not have been ready to share everything, but the very act of sharing his passion with us was a gift in itself. Even if he didn't realise it, his excitement was an offering that spoke volumes about his desire for connection, even as he kept parts of himself safely tucked away.

And just like that, Gout was gone again. The energy shifted as he rushed off to tend to a bathroom mess caused by another patient's discomfort. The urgency in his movements was palpable, a reminder that life in the hospital was a constant balancing act between the need for privacy and the demands of survival.

Physically absent, Gout's presence still lingered in the room, like the echo of a conversation that continued long after the words had stopped. He was struggling, wrestling with emotional baggage that he wasn't yet ready to release. There was so much he needed to let go of before he could truly move forward, before he could stand on his own two feet, metaphorically and literally, and break free from the confines of his wheelchair.

Gout's story, like so many of ours, was not just about the physical body or external circumstances. It was about the internal battles we fight, the emotional walls we build, and the long journey towards freedom and healing. The release process isn't just about the things we can touch; it's about the things we can't see, the weight of unspoken words, unresolved pain, and untold stories. Gout wasn't ready to share all of himself yet, but in his small acts of connection, he was beginning to open the door to a future where he could.

Setting the Standard

The Nursing Unit Manager (NUM) had promised to sit down with me by the end of the day to discuss the Partnering with Consumer Standard, a framework meant to ensure my voice and experience were heard. But as the day wore on, the promise went unfulfilled. She later informed me that any complaints about perceived intimidation should be directed to her. I waited patiently, hoping for a shift, for a meaningful conversation. But when I asked when I could speak with her, I was told she had gone home and wouldn't be back until Monday. Another promise left unkept. Another layer of frustration. Another crack in my belief that anything could change here.

On Monday, during the morning meeting, an opportunity for consumers to have a say, I once again asked about the process for speaking with the NUM. The response was perfunctory: "Tell your nurse, and they'll follow up." I wondered whether displaying the process somewhere for all consumers to view would be possible. A visual guide could empower us, clarify processes, and ensure no one felt lost in the system. It could be a small step towards transparency, a gesture of respect towards those seeking to advocate for themselves.

I had been hoping for mediation with the nurse I found intimidating, the one who had once told me, "You know where you are," as if the statement alone should settle any disquiet. But it didn't. It only amplified the tension, reminding me of my physical presence in a place where I didn't feel safe or supported. This was the same nurse who had substituted decision-making for Generosity, disregarding my voice. I didn't need to be reminded of where I was; I needed to be treated with dignity and to feel heard and understood. The NUM had promised to organise a time for mediation, but that promise, too, went unfulfilled. Again, the empty echo of frustration and anger reverberated in my chest.

This experience has shown me more than just a lack of follow-through; it has revealed the reality of being in a place where the system is more concerned with maintaining control than offering genuine care. Now, I truly know where I am: a place where promises are broken, where emotional support is a distant dream, and where the only therapeutic tool at my disposal is journaling. Here, amidst the company of other patients, I have no access to the basic services that should be standard in any healthcare facility, services that respect my humanity and my rights.

The conditions here have become a reflection of neglect. My nails grow increasingly unkempt because nail clippers are inaccessible. The hygiene of the showers is questionable at best, leading to a contracted case of tinea. Even when I lock my door, someone can still access my belongings without permission. In this place, the physical and emotional landscapes are neglected, leaving me to navigate the void between the promises made and the reality I experience daily.

I don't need reminders of my location. I've lived through this reality for weeks, where nothing changes and every day feels the same. The lack of care and the absence of real action make me wonder if this is what I can expect from a system designed to heal. But no matter where I am, I am still a human being with human rights. The right to be treated with respect. The right to feel safe. The right to have my voice heard. These rights should not be contingent upon where I am or the whims of those who are supposed to help me. They are my birthright, and I will continue to claim them, even here.

Going Home Scares Her

ECT was not yet ready to leave. The very thought of returning home terrified her. She feared the uncertainty of homelessness or the possibility of going back to a place filled with painful memories of domestic violence. The weight of her past loomed over her, keeping her anchored in a place of fear and indecision.

I suggested different possibilities, hoping to help her envision a path forward. Renting a property, exploring house-sharing options, or even temporarily staying in a caravan park until she found work all seemed like viable steps towards reclaiming stability. I also offered the idea of surrounding herself with tech experts, a community where she could find support as she secured a job in her field of expertise. The world was filled with opportunities, but she wasn't ready to seize them.

She didn't act on any of these ideas. No searches were made, and no enquiries were pursued. The inertia was palpable, as if the fear of failure or the discomfort of change kept her from exploring her options. Instead, she grew angrier and more anxious. The Aboriginal Liaison Officer tried to ease her anxiety, but even their calm presence couldn't cut through the storm of her emotions. She wasn't prepared to listen to advice or take steps to move forward. The possibilities felt overwhelming, and the fear of what might lie beyond her reality seemed insurmountable.

ECT wasn't ready to heal. Her anger and anxiety were a barrier, an emotional armour she wasn't yet willing to let go of. As much as the healthcare system tried to support her, and as much as I wanted to help her see the potential within herself, the truth was that she wasn't ready to trust in her ability to change. She wasn't prepared to let go of the complicated past that had shaped her, nor to take responsibility for the future she could still create. Without trust and the willingness to take the first step, healing was impossible.

She wasn't ready yet, and that was okay. Sometimes the healing journey requires more than just practical steps. It requires emotional readiness, the courage to face fear, and the willingness to trust in the process. Until then, she would remain where she was, caught in the cycle of anxiety and anger. And while I could offer support and ideas, the decision to take control and heal had to come from within her.

A Parting Gift

Throughout my time in the hospital, I was often directed to speak with the team leader or the Nursing Unit Manager (NUM), but each time I found myself waiting in vain. I was told to talk to my nurse during the morning meeting, the onetime consumers were supposed to have direct access to the nurses. But when I tried, I was advised not to speak to my nurse, as I was allegedly being disciplined for bullying her. At that moment, I was reminded again of how unheard I felt in this place.

This was the same hospital where I was labelled an "arrogant pig" for wanting to be treated as an equal, a partner in my care. This was the same hospital where a fellow patient was made to feel intimidated simply for asking to understand his rights. There was a distinct feeling that my voice didn't matter.

Still, I tried to reach out despite the resistance. I didn't trust my nurse, so I approached six other nurses, each telling me to have breakfast first. So I went to breakfast, unsure whether to laugh or cry at the absurdity.

As I sat there, I spotted the team leader through a window. He had never once spoken to me before, and I only recognised him after someone pointed him out. He signalled that he would talk to me in ten minutes. I waited. I returned in ten, twenty, then thirty minutes, but he never came.

Now, I sit here, writing. Writing because it feels like the only way to make sense of a world that has so often been filled with empty promises, unmet expectations, and frustration. I asked another nurse if I could speak with someone. She told me he was in his office. But once again, he refused to come out to see me. Another promise was broken. More frustration. More anger.

But as I sit with my feelings, I realise this is not the end. This hospital experience, though marked by neglect, has also been a part of my journey. It has shown me the power of my voice, even when it feels silenced. It has reminded me that I am worthy of being heard, respected, and honoured.

Perhaps this chapter is not just about the absence of care, but also about the beginning of learning how to stand up for myself, create space for my voice, and understand that the healing process is often messy and difficult. The parting gift this hospital gave me, though not in the form of support or kindness from the staff, was the realisation that I am responsible for my own healing, journey, and voice. It is a gift I will carry as I step forward into whatever comes next.

Isolation

Yesterday, one of our friends, overwhelmed by the crushing weight of her frustration, punched a nurse. It was a reaction borne of weeks of isolation, a silent scream in response to the emotional turmoil she had endured. She had been confined to a room for over a week, isolated due to COVID-19, and amid that isolation, she had lost her daughter.

She longed to return home to the familiar space where she felt she might regain some semblance of control over her life, but now her outburst has led to criminal charges being filed against her. She is a petite woman, physically small, yet the emotional weight she carried seemed to make her appear much larger than life. We watched as she reached her breaking point, her screams echoing through the sterile halls, a desperate plea for understanding as nurses and security guards surrounded her. She was cornered, both physically and emotionally.

At that moment, I felt the weight of her isolation as though it were my own. There was nothing I could do to protect her from the system that failed her, nothing I could say to ease her pain. We were powerless in the face of her suffering. I could only watch as they restrained her, the violence of the situation overshadowing the cries for compassion that hung in the air.

She needed a hug, a simple act of human connection, but all she received was a message that it was not her fault, a message that, in the end, felt hollow. It wasn't her fault, but the fault of a system that isolated her, stripped her of her dignity, and failed to acknowledge the human behind the label.

Isolation is cruel. It chips away at a person's sense of self-worth and emotional balance. In her struggle, I saw how deeply a lack of connection can wound. In those moments of isolation, we are cut off from human support and understanding, and our most vulnerable parts are exposed. And yet, even then, I knew that real healing begins with connection, something she was denied.

As I reflect on her pain, I am reminded of the power of compassion. Sometimes, all a person truly needs is to be seen, heard, and know that they are not alone. Yet isolation is often the response in a place meant for healing.

In my heart, I know that the healing journey must begin with recognising every individual's inherent worth and dignity. It must start with a human connection, something that walls, security, or labels can never replace.

Gout Goes Off

Gout becomes increasingly agitated, and the weight of the noise seems to press down on him, squeezing the last vestiges of his patience. Our friend in the room next door, isolated from the world, has set off her alarm again, a constant and jarring reminder of her distress. The nurses cannot stop the unrelenting sound, and Gout, who is sensitive to sensory overload, reaches his breaking point.

He asks for the alarm to be turned off, but his words go unheard. He yells, his voice rising in frustration, echoing off the sterile walls. He bangs on the door, desperate for someone to hear him and help. But no one comes. The alarm blares uninterrupted as time stretches into an unbearable eternity. Three hours pass, and the noise continues, a reminder of the helplessness that has come to define this place.

Gout, overwhelmed and exhausted by the sensory assault, receives a jab. He is told to "calm down", as though his distress were something he could control with a thought, as though mere words could quiet the noise that pierces his very being. We, his friends, are instructed to leave him alone, step back, and let them handle it. All we can do is watch as they attempt to calm him with another needle, another dose to numb the anguish that has taken root in his heart.

He cries. Tears spill down his face, not from weakness but from a depth of pain that no medication can touch. I watch him, my heart heavy, as I see the joy he had yesterday gone. All he wanted, all he asked for, was for the alarm to be turned off, for the relentless assault on his senses to stop. But it continues. The alarm never stops.

At that moment, I feel the weight of his suffering. It is not just the noise, but the crushing feeling of being ignored, the agony of being seen as nothing more than a problem to be managed. We are not people to them; we are cases, statistics, and bodies to be medicated and controlled. But Gout's pain, his humanity, is real. It is raw. It is unrelenting. And in the face of it, I am left with an aching sense of futility.

In this place, where healing is supposed to happen, where care is meant to be provided, it seems that the only thing that persists is the noise: the noise of suffering, the noise of frustration, the noise of lives lost to a system that fails to see us for who we truly are.

Intimidation Walks Me Out

Sensing my agitation, the nurses could see the storm brewing inside me. They knew I was on the verge of losing it, of breaking free somehow, so they informed me that my papers were complete. My release was imminent; the next chapter of my journey awaited at The Hills Clinic. Intimidation, my assigned nurse for the day, came to unlock my door. She led me to gather my things, and I hugged my friends, feeling the warmth of their support one last time before I stepped into the unknown.

Then Intimidation walked me towards a door that had been locked to me for three and a half weeks, a door I had longed to pass through but had never been allowed to. With my bags in hand, I stepped forward, taking my first step into freedom. The irony wasn't lost on me. Intimidation, which had often loomed over me, was now guiding me out. It felt like a quiet victory, a subtle reversal of power, even as I left the sterile walls of the hospital behind.

As I walked out the door, I couldn't help but look back, the weight of the experience pressing against my chest. I never wanted to set foot in that psychiatric facility again. I couldn't. The memory of being held captive, of being surrounded by others who were also confined, detainees in their own right, each battling their demons, was too much. It had been a place where time stood still, where every day felt like a struggle to maintain any semblance of sanity.

And just like that, I was free. I stepped away from the madness of the place, leaving behind the twisted system that had kept me locked in a cycle of care that never truly healed and never truly understood. I walked out, and I could breathe for the first time in a long while. The path ahead was uncertain, but it was mine to walk. No more locked doors. No more empty promises. Just the world, waiting for me to reclaim my place in it.

The Hills

As I drove toward the Hills Clinic, agitation bubbled inside me. I had asked my Best Friend to drive me since I was still not speaking to my parents, and she had been handling all the logistical details between them. But the trip quickly took a turn for the worse. Old grievances resurfaced, and we exchanged heated words throughout the journey. After all, I had hurt her deeply. I had cheated on her and treated her terribly, and the tension between us was palpable. The air was thick with unspoken resentments, and what should have been a smooth transition was marred by the weight of our unresolved issues.

Even though I struggled with my relationship with my Best Friend, I was also in the final days of my bond with the Goddess. She was growing increasingly concerned about my chaotic and unpredictable mania. She didn't understand why I had chosen my Best Friend to be my next of kin, especially given that my focus seemed to remain on my ex-girlfriend. With the Goddess's growing concerns, I decided to name her as my joint carer on my Carers Statement at the Hills.

Arriving at the Hills was a breath of fresh air. The atmosphere was warm, welcoming, and vastly different from my experience at Nepean Hospital. Smiles greeted me at the door, and I immediately felt an energy shift. Within moments of arrival, I began filling out my Collaborative Care Plan, and within a day, I had a Treatment Plan in place. It was a stark contrast to the lack of planning at Nepean, where I had been left in the dark about my care, my treatment, and my future. At Nepean, I had left feeling just as manic as when I had arrived, without any structure to guide me. I had felt lost, unable to work through the affective symptoms that were exacerbating my mental health struggles.

Though the transition was far from easy, the Hills offered me desperately needed support. For the first two weeks, I remained agitated and hypervigilant. My psychiatrist, aware of my condition, expressed concern that I was still in a hypomanic state and ensured that the nursing staff kept a close watch on me. I was struggling with the trauma of my recent experiences at Nepean, where I had reached my breaking point while witnessing the decline of others around me. The lingering feeling of intimidation was hard to shake. The fear and uncertainty of being in a vulnerable state were overwhelming at times, and it took a while for me to feel even remotely comfortable. By evening, around 8:00 pm, I would find myself gripped by such intense agitation that relaxation seemed impossible. It was as if my body and mind refused to calm down. The prescribed medication, including increased Seroquel, sometimes wasn't enough, and I resorted to benzodiazepines to force myself into sleep.

Despite the turbulence, I made the most of my time at the Hills. The food was nourishing, and I began filling my days with activities that helped ground me. I engaged in Tai Chi and martial arts and attended the gym sessions when they were available. I attended therapy classes, learning valuable techniques such as Cognitive Behavioural Therapy (CBT), Acceptance and Commitment Therapy (ACT), and Dialectical Behaviour Therapy (DBT). These tools were invaluable in giving me strategies for managing my mental health. I also explored diet, gut health, and their impact on mental well-being. I took long walks every day, sometimes alone and sometimes with other residents. The fresh air and exercise were grounding and therapeutic.

I had a comfortable room with an ensuite, a space I could finally call my own. The nursing staff were supportive and genuinely cared about my recovery. The people at the Hills were kind and welcoming, and it felt far removed from the cold, clinical environment I had just left behind.

With access to my computer, I started to write. I pieced together my story from my time in hospital. Within a few manic bursts of energy, I sketched out most of this book. The act of writing became a form of therapy in itself, a way for me to process the trauma of my past. As the days passed, I began working on my "trauma years," trying to make sense of the events that had shaped my mental health struggles. By the end of my three-and-a-half-week stay, I had written the outline for my memoirs, detailing the pain and growth that had brought me to this point. I wrote four or five chapters daily, pouring my heart into the pages.

As I settled in, my mania began to subside, and my agitation gradually diminished. The adjustment to a new medication regimen was making a noticeable difference in my mood fluctuations. My psychiatrist acknowledged my progress and revised my diagnosis to reflect a more accurate picture: schizoaffective disorder. This new diagnosis felt like a small step toward understanding myself more clearly. The Hills had been a highly productive environment for me, filled with growth, learning, and healing. I now had a set of tools to apply in the real world, which I had already begun using to rebuild my life. The next step was simple: to put them into practice.

The Creation Story

The entire experience had been a wild ride, a journey that seemed to unfold like a living creation story. It all began at One Door, a time marked by various experiences in Newcastle that pushed me to the brink of insanity. Eventually, I found myself elated in Richmond, yet ironically, I had lost my mind. In my thoughts, I was living out what I had envisioned as my "Creation Story."

However, this idea of living out my Creation Story was a delusion rooted in years of deep research. I had spent countless hours studying physics, biology, and religion, creating extensive documents and presentations on evolution and creation titled *The Evolutionary History of Creation.* This body of work had occupied my mind for years, and as my mania deepened, I began to perceive my life as a continuation of this evolutionary narrative.

As my delusion evolved, I became convinced that the fourth day of my "evolutionary" story, the day of paranoid reptiles, would mark the "last day" of humanity. In my vision, only a small portion of humans would survive to bring forth a "New Dawn," and my death would signal the apocalyptic war that, in my mind, was necessary for humanity's next phase of evolution. I believed that the New Dawn would end the chaos of the "Fourth Day" and lead to the next stages of human development: an era of "experiencing emotions" followed by an era of "understanding thoughts" and "contextualising" the evolution story.

Here's how I understood the evolutionary process at the time:

- **Day 1: Creation of the physical world and technology.** I believed I was immersing myself in technology, creating a business to form a platform that would unite humanity's greatest minds. I even thought Elon Musk needed to send me into space so I could be frozen in time, setting the universe into perpetual motion. My belief that I was the focal point of creation was bolstered by a delusion that my body in space would unite the universe for eternity at the end of the seven days.

- **Day 2: Creation of Earth and the struggle between land, sea, and sky.** I thought the world was on the brink of collapse due to environmental destruction, believing it was my mission to unite Heaven (me) and Earth (humanity) to avoid total extinction. In my delusion, I sent letters to Elon Musk and others, claiming that my platform and my work on evolution would be key to the survival of humanity and to ushering in the "New Dawn."
- **Day 3: Life is brought to the story as simple cells evolve.** This was the day I believed life would begin to take shape, not just on Earth but in the evolution of humanity itself. The chaos of my delusion seemed to come together in what I believed was a magical way as I delved into creating the concept of a higher power.
- **Day 4: The evolution of paranoid, obsessive, compulsive reptiles.** This day marked the height of my anxiety and paranoia. I thought the apocalyptic war would end and give way to a more peaceful time. As I saw it, the world's struggles were part of the evolutionary process that would lead to ultimate peace and the "New Dawn."
- **Day 5: Mammals evolve emotions.** I believed this day would begin a new emotional era in which humanity would finally learn to express emotions freely. I even thought I was teaching those around me in the hospital profound lessons on emotions, as if guiding them toward this new way of being.
- **Day 6: Humans evolve through thought, self-talk, and imagination.** I envisioned this era as one in which humanity would use science and technology to contextualise all experiences. I believed my work on my computer and the platform I had created would lead to a renaissance of knowledge that could solve any problem in the universe.

- **Day 7: The rest of the story evolves.** In my mind, the final day would be the culmination of this evolutionary journey, where the universe would align and enter perpetual motion, completing the cycle of creation.

As the story played out in my life, I tried to match each day of the creation sequence to my daily experiences:

- Day 1: I purchased significant technology, believing I was embarking on an evolutionary adventure.
- Day 2: I travelled with friends and drafted a letter to Elon Musk about humanity's predicament.
- Day 3: I formulated my understanding of a Higher Power, but had a psychotic break that night.
- Day 4: I woke up with the revelation that I was the creator of my own story and preached this idea, only to be followed by the police and eventually hospitalised.
- Day 5: I spent most of the day in the high-dependency unit, fighting for my rights and trying to make sense of my delusions.
- Day 6: I focused on advocating for myself in the high-dependency unit, feeling unheard and frustrated.
- Day 7: The rest of the story unfolds in this book.

Throughout this experience, I attempted to live out my creation myth, to bring order to the chaos that consumed my mind. The key themes of my journey, the interplay between mind and reality, the struggle for understanding, the need for emotional expression, and the search for meaning in an evolving universe, came to the forefront of my delusion. Yet what I eventually came to realise is that, while my delusions had shaped my experience, they also highlighted a deep desire for self-understanding and an attempt to make sense of the world around me.

Ultimately, the journey was not just a descent into madness but a reflection of a deeper spiritual quest, a quest that, in its most chaotic form, was still rooted in the search for wholeness and truth within the fabric of the universe.

Fighting for My Rights

From 2 January to 26 January 2023, I found myself in a public psychiatric ward, caught in the grips of a manic high and a psychotic state. The environment was thick with trauma and delusions, creating a distressing atmosphere not only for me but for the other patients as well. With little support from the nursing staff and limited activities to help pass the time, the hospital's tense atmosphere was far from conducive to healing.

As someone with extensive experience as a consumer advocate striving to improve conditions in public mental health facilities, I was disheartened by what I encountered. The situation seemed to have deteriorated compared to my previous hospitalisation 20 years prior, and the lack of meaningful activities or even basic opportunities for walks only intensified the stress of the experience.

One of the most disappointing aspects was the scarcity of peer worker visits, only one during my three-and-a-half-week stay. Given the nursing staff's reluctance to engage and the infrequency of social worker interactions, peer workers could have provided much-needed professional support for patients navigating their traumatic and stressful circumstances. Patients dealing with extensive trauma and complex needs could have greatly benefited from the understanding and guidance that peer workers are uniquely equipped to provide.

Leaving the hospital, I couldn't help but feel disheartened by the state of mental health care. Despite efforts to improve conditions and increase the accessibility of peer work, the reality I faced was all too familiar. The staff focused on control rather than patient collaboration, and the support available was woefully inadequate.

Nevertheless, amid the turmoil and frustration, I found moments of solace and understanding. Reflecting on the months leading up to my hospitalisation, I began to recognise the emotional highs and lows that had affected my life. I acknowledged the importance of seeking strategies to cope with these fluctuations.

I now feel a renewed sense of purpose and determination emerging from the hospital. While my journey is far from over, I am prepared to face the challenges ahead. I am committed to taking control of my life, seeking the necessary support, and continuing to advocate for improved mental health care, both for myself and others navigating similar struggles.

The Dialectics of Mania

In *The Dialectics of Mania*, I have explored the complex interplay between mental health, self-advocacy, and the broader systemic challenges that affect those experiencing mental illness. Through my journey, I have encountered the dualities of existence, joy and suffering, strength and vulnerability, revealing how they are often intertwined in the experience of mania and mental health crises.

The book reflects on the ongoing tension between the individual's internal struggle and the external systems designed to provide support. It underscores the limitations of psychiatric care, particularly in public mental health settings, where institutionalised approaches often prioritise control over true partnership and healing. Despite these challenges, the narrative also highlights the profound resilience of the human spirit, the importance of self-awareness, and the potential for transformation even within oppressive environments.

A key theme that has emerged throughout my exploration is recognising the cyclical nature of mental health. Like all emotional states, mania is not static but flows through phases of intensity and calm. I have learned that, while these fluctuations can be destabilising, they also offer opportunities for growth and self-discovery, provided we approach them with compassion, awareness, and a willingness to confront the complexities of our inner lives.

Equally significant is the role of peer support and self-advocacy in navigating the mental health system. My journey has reaffirmed the need for a collaborative, empathetic approach to care, one that values individuals' lived experiences and fosters genuine connections between patients and caregivers. The book emphasises that true healing comes not from control but from partnership, respect, and the integration of professional and peer support networks.

Ultimately, my journey through mania and the mental health system has taught me that healing is an ongoing process. It requires pursuing external support and an internal reckoning with our fears, desires, and vulnerabilities. The lessons of self-compassion, advocacy, and resilience are fundamental to navigating the complexities of mental health. As I continue on this path, I am committed to deepening my understanding of myself, advocating for systemic change, and supporting others in their journeys toward healing and self-empowerment.

In closing, *The Dialectics of Mania* is not just a personal account but a broader reflection on the dynamics of mental health care, the need for systemic transformation, and the power of human connection. It is an invitation to recognise the complexity of our experiences and the potential for growth within even the most challenging circumstances.

Scorecard for Nepean Psychiatric Hospital

Copy Provided to Consumer	**Yes**	**No**	**Comment**
I have been fully informed about my rights and responsibilities.		X	Only four patients received a rights statement. Only one had a staff member go through it, and it was done so intimidatingly that the patient said, "I will be scared of you now." The staff responded, "Good, that's how it should be."
Receipt of consumer package		X	I received this on my last day in my locker. No one went through it with me.
I have been informed of peer support options.		X	No one knew about peer support options. When I asked a nurse about it, I was told, "You are not here to help other participants."
People who have helped me with this plan		Nil	I completed this plan myself on the fourth day of admission. No one else was informed that a Wellness Plan was available.

Mental Health Carer Experience Survey		Nil	My carer was never asked to complete this survey. I found it in the visitor room. No one told her it was available.
Your experience of (YES) Service	X		I filled this out around day twenty. Although the service is better than 20 years ago, I expressed how poor it still is. There is a long way to go to change the Us vs. Them culture and improve partnership with consumers.

Letter to the Local Member

Dear Susan,

I have a lot of respect for you and the work you do for the Macquarie electorate. You are the best member we have ever had. I am currently in the acute ward of Nepean Hospital.

I reached my tipping point last night and lost it. I have been calm and relaxed until the last few days, but have become increasingly anxious as I feel unheard and disrespected by most of the staff. Even the most straightforward requests, like asking for a pen, seem difficult. In addition, I have been lied to on numerous occasions. Do not get me wrong, the conditions are significantly better than my stay in Pialla in 2003, but there is still an 'Us vs Them' culture between the staff and 'consumers.' Since arriving at the hospital nearly three and a half weeks ago, the diversional therapist has visited four times. I was grateful that I got to make tie-dye bags, play the keyboard for a bit, and have an opportunity to do some art, and today I had a little play with Play-Doh.

The dietitian sat down with me for five minutes to do a nutritional screen and gave me some excellen-t nutritional resources, for which I was grateful. The social worker came around yesterday and talked to some of the clients, which was great, but these clients have complex needs with the NDIS, Centrelink, housing, and more. One visit in three weeks is ridiculous and appalling, to be honest. The Medical Superintendent visited me on the day I requested, which I greatly appreciated. I respected his advice at the time. Apart from that, however, I have received little or no support, no therapy, and limited assistance from the nursing staff. My five minutes with the pastor were a complete waste of time.

After a week here, I had the much-needed rest I required to get my mental health back to a state of balance. Many of my physical markers have stabilised. My psychiatrist told me at the time that I had progressed enough and was in a stable state of mind to get the support I required. But when I rang the Hills Clinic, where she said she would send a referral, no referral had been sent. Yesterday, my psychiatrist refused to let me leave because I was still scheduled as a 'mentally ill' patient. I am unsure how she came to this conclusion, as she has not asked me any questions about my mental health. I have never had any assessment, not even a K-10, or any baseline to see if my mental health is improving. I have now been in this hospital for nearly three weeks. I have not seen a tree for three weeks.

I have had to pace up and down the same corridor and the small courtyard to keep my steps up. I have been unable to go for a drive to unwind. I have been unable to go to a café to get my morning coffee. I would love to go to a restaurant to have a nice meal. I am happy with the hospital food, but I am sure you take the simple luxuries I cannot for granted. How would your mental health be if you were denied many things you take for granted?

Overall, morale in this place has been good because of the support the patients provide each other. Many have extensive trauma, which can get overwhelming at times. The nurses seem reluctant to help.

I have informed many staff members about Standard 2, Partnering with Consumers, the guidelines that the Australian Quality and Safeguards Commission expects all hospitals in Australia to base their operational procedures on. In particular, I have asked them to print off the 'Collaborative Care' standard that focuses on working together on a care plan in collaboration between staff and 'us' consumers. Unfortunately, I was told numerous times that they could not find this document on the internet, despite me finding the guidelines within seconds through a simple Google search once I finally had access to my phone after difficulties with it.

When one of my fellow patients asked to review his rights, the nurse did so in an intimidating way that led the patient to say, 'I am afraid of you now!' The nurse responded, 'Good, that's how it should be.' I have brought this to the attention of the Official Visitors, who I hope will address this issue through the necessary channels to make such intimidating behaviour unacceptable.

I was told I was 'an arrogant pig', or something to that effect, because I asked to review the Partnering with Consumers Standard with a nurse, hoping to go through a collaborative care plan as highlighted in the standard. So who is the arrogant one? The person who wants to be a partner in his own care, or the person who thinks he knows his role so well that he is unwilling to improve his professional practice in line with best practice recommended by the Australian Government?

There is no way to get better in the hospital. There is little stimulation on the ward besides a boxing bag and a few pieces of exercise equipment. I do not smoke, but many patients need a cigarette or two a day to remain calm. Since this is off-limits, many patients resort to more addictive methods to calm down, such as Valium. Boredom and frustration often lead to outbursts, many of which are ignored. Some patients have been injected as a last resort due to frustration. They are not being heard. How are we supposed to improve our mental health with such little stimulation?

Many nursing staff seem too busy with paperwork to spend meaningful time with us. For example, I completed a wellness plan, but when I asked other patients during a morning meeting, the only opportunity they have each day to express their concerns, no one knew this was available.

When I asked how many people had received a Rights Statement, a fundamental human right and policy of this hospital, only four had. I was one of the advocates who fought for this Rights Statement to be instated upon admission. I first received my Rights Statement on my third day in the hospital, and I only received it after another patient alerted me that they had received a statement of their rights.

I have conducted an online seminar with international leaders on the Rights of Persons with Disability. I am a published author on supported and substituted decision-making about Legal Capacity. I fought for five months to obtain the documents from my first, highly traumatic stay at Pialla, where I was abused by being given 15 DIFFERENT medications in the first two days of my hospital stay. I know my rights under the Freedoms of Information Act. I conduct presentations to groups about Consumer Rights. I know my Rights.

You know a little about me, but I need a lot of mental stimulation to stay well. Physical exercise is essential for my well-being, and music helps keep me calm. Unfortunately, I cannot access my computer to do any meaningful work. My current exercise consists of taking my steps within the corridors and courtyard of the ward. I have not had any opportunity to play my piano other than about half an hour on a faulty keyboard. How am I supposed to stay calm or express myself when I cannot access the things that keep me well? How would your mental health be if you could not access anything essential to your well-being?

One final thing for you to consider.

I have seen my girlfriend in person for two hours over the last three weeks. Imagine spending two hours with your partner, unable to hug, kiss, or wake up next to them. Imagine being unable to go home to the loved ones who give you comfort, happiness, and joy. Because I am 'mentally ill' without being diagnosed through objective or subjective criteria, does that mean we do not need love, touch, compassion, or happiness with our loved ones?

I have written down many of my colleagues' and staff's concerns and ways this place could improve. It is essential to ensure that all mental health facilities one day follow the standards recommended by the Australian Government.

I am safe here and hope to be heard, but I am losing hope. It is every person's right to be heard, and I have not felt heard during my stay in this hospital. I hope to work together to ensure standards are practised in all mental health facilities in Australia and worldwide.

I hope you are having a cracking 2023.

BLOG 1: Trust Beyond the Exercises: Building Lasting Bonds

Trust is a fundamental pillar of human relationships and is essential for fostering genuine connections. In many environments, such as the workplace or therapeutic settings, trust exercises are commonly used to help people bond and establish a sense of trust. However, the question remains: do these exercises truly reflect the complexities of trust, or do they merely offer temporary camaraderie?

Trust exercises often involve vulnerability, such as leaning back and relying on someone to catch you before you fall. While such activities can create an immediate sense of connection and trust, they do not necessarily provide a comprehensive picture of the depth and intricacy of human relationships.

Building and maintaining trust goes far beyond just catching someone in an exercise. It requires consistency, openness, and a willingness to be vulnerable over time. The following points delve deeper into the essential components of trust that extend beyond simple exercises:

1. **Communication:** Open and honest communication is the backbone of trust. Being transparent about your thoughts, feelings, and intentions is essential to creating a solid foundation of trust in any relationship.
2. **Reliability:** Consistency in words and actions is crucial for trust. If you commit to something, follow through, as this demonstrates to others that you can be counted on.
3. **Empathy:** Showing understanding and compassion towards others' feelings and experiences is vital to trust. When people

feel heard and validated, they are more likely to open up and trust others.

4. **Integrity:** Align your actions with your values and beliefs. Trust is built when people see that you are genuine to yourself.
5. **Acceptance:** Trust often involves embracing others for who they are, without judgement or expectation. By accepting others, we create a space for trust to flourish.
6. **Forgiveness:** Trust can be fragile, and misunderstandings or mistakes can cause it to waver. Being willing to forgive and move forward is essential in sustaining trust over time.

In conclusion, while trust exercises can be a valuable starting point for establishing connections, it is important to recognise that they represent only a small part of the trust-building process. Developing and nurturing lasting trust requires ongoing effort, vulnerability, and a commitment to understanding and supporting one another. By focusing on the essential components of trust, we can cultivate deeper, more meaningful connections that stand the test of time.

BLOG 2: Navigating the Maze: My Experience with the Mental Health System

As someone who has experienced the mental health system first-hand, I understand the frustration and confusion that can arise while navigating it. In this blog post, I share my journey through the system, shedding light on my challenges and the importance of advocating for one's rights.

It all began when I entered the hospital, seeking help and hoping to start a treatment plan. I waited hours in various areas, from the Triage and Assessment Centre (TAC) to the emergency department, before being transferred to the High Dependency Unit (HDU). Throughout this entire process, I was repeatedly told that I would see a psychiatrist soon.

However, as time wore on, the wait grew increasingly frustrating. I learned from other patients, such as Black Magic and The Hacker, that they had been waiting for days, even weeks, without seeing a doctor or psychiatrist. It became apparent that something was amiss within the system.

The Hacker introduced me to the Rights Statement, a document outlining patients' rights that I had once advocated for. Ironically, I had not received this statement upon my admission. The Rights Statement clarified patients' rights to see medical personnel within 12 hours of being admitted and to be assessed by a medical specialist every 24 hours.

Realising that my rights were not being respected, I demanded to see the Medical Superintendent, as permitted under the Rights Statement. The response I received was less than satisfactory. I was told to submit my request in writing, with the caveat that the Superintendent was extremely busy and might not respond for days.

Refusing to be deterred, I learned about the Official Visitors, individuals who visit hospitals monthly to address concerns, complaints, or positive patient feedback. As luck would have it, they were scheduled to visit that afternoon.

My experience navigating the mental health system was riddled with delays, misinformation, and frustration. It highlighted the importance of advocating for one's rights and remaining persistent in adversity. By sharing my story, I hope to encourage others to stand up for their rights and work towards improving the mental health system for all who rely on it.

BLOG 3: Fighting for Mental Health Care Rights: A Personal Journey Through a Flawed System

In a world where mental health is increasingly gaining attention, patients must receive the care they deserve. This is my journey advocating for my rights while detained in a mental health facility and the struggle I faced in obtaining the proper care I needed.

My story began on 3 January 2023, when I was admitted to the High Dependency Unit of a mental health facility. I expected that the necessary legal procedures would be followed and that I would receive timely care from the medical staff. However, my experience was far from ideal.

According to Schedule 3, the Statement of Rights for Persons Detained in Mental Health Facilities, patients must be seen by a facility doctor no later than 12 hours after arrival. In my case, I waited over 23 hours without being seen by any medical personnel. Despite my growing frustration, I remained patient and hopeful that I would eventually receive the care I needed.

In pursuing justice and proper treatment, I carefully reviewed my rights statement and contacted Law Access NSW for guidance. Unfortunately, they could not provide legal advice but offered three alternative phone numbers for further assistance. All I wanted was the right care to help me recover.

Throughout my time at the facility, I encountered numerous obstacles in my pursuit of adequate care. Some nurses seemed dismissive, unbothered by the fact that my legal rights were being breached. In one instance, when I inquired about the delay in seeing a doctor, a nurse shut the door in my face, further exacerbating my sense of helplessness.

My goal was not to claim that I was completely 'well' but rather to find the best possible care to aid my recovery. I strongly believed that the Ramsey Clinic, where I had received exemplary care in the past, was the right place for me. My plea to the Medical Superintendent was simple: I sought proper care and attention for my mental health condition and was prepared to take legal action if my rights continued to be disregarded.

This blog post serves as a testament to my experience, shedding light on the importance of fighting for one's mental health care rights. It is crucial that patients are treated with respect and dignity and that the mental health care system becomes more accountable in providing the care that individuals so desperately need.

BLOG 4: The Struggle for Trust and Understanding in Mental Health Facilities

We seek comfort, understanding, and support in our most vulnerable moments. Mental health facilities are designed to be havens for healing, where individuals grappling with psychological challenges can find solace and professional guidance. However, at times, these institutions can leave us feeling even more isolated and afraid.

Imagine the anxiety and frustration of waiting hours, even days, to speak with a psychiatrist when your emotional turmoil is at its peak. Your rights statement assures you that a professional will see you within 12 hours of arrival, yet that time comes and goes without any sign of the help you so desperately need. You are met with condescension and dismissal when you question the delay, as if your needs and rights are insignificant.

During these trying times, empathy from staff in mental health facilities is crucial. It is disheartening to see fellow patients, such as Black Magic, who are dealing with severe conditions like schizophrenia, being treated with intimidation and disdain. Instead of receiving the support they need, they feel threatened and fearful of seeking help.

Nurses and other mental health professionals should foster an environment of trust and understanding rather than instilling fear and apprehension in the people they are meant to help. It is essential to recognise that patients are in these facilities because they are struggling and require professional care to navigate their journey towards healing.

A single dismissive or intimidating interaction can leave lasting emotional scars on patients who are already grappling with severe mental health challenges. It is time for mental health facilities to prioritise empathy, compassion, and genuine understanding of their patients' struggles. By doing so, they can create an environment where trust and healing can truly flourish.

BLOG 5: Finding Peace of Mind: The Power of Advocacy and the Official Visitors Program

In a world where mental health patients often feel unheard and marginalised, the Official Visitors Program plays a crucial role in bridging the gap between patients and decision-makers. As a patient advocate, I have witnessed firsthand the importance of effective communication and ensuring patients' rights are respected in mental health facilities.

My experience at St John of God Hospital as a Consumer Advisory Partners Committee (CAPC) member allowed me to gather patient feedback and relay their concerns to the executive committee. This process facilitated positive changes and fostered open communication between patients and hospital administrators. Similarly, the Official Visitors Program advocates for change at the service and systems level across hospitals in New South Wales.

During a particularly frustrating time in my treatment journey, I encountered the Official Visitors themselves. The hospital's feedback box was inaccessible, so they sat with me and discussed my concerns. We spoke at length about violations of patients' rights, the intimidation some patients felt when inquiring about their rights, and the importance of adhering to the Partners in Consumer Standards set by the Australian Quality and Safety Commission.

Their compassion and genuine interest in my concerns validated my feelings. They reassured me that they would work to ensure the hospital recognised the significance of upholding rights, laws, and standards for patient wellbeing. This encounter brought me peace of mind and highlighted the critical role played by programs like the Official Visitors in mental health care.

By advocating for patients and holding mental health facilities accountable, the Official Visitors Program helps create a more supportive and empathetic environment for patients to heal. As patients, knowing that people are fighting for our rights and working to improve our treatment experiences is empowering and comforting, a vital component in the journey towards recovery.

BLOG 6: Reclaiming Power Through Vulnerability: A Journey to Healing

There are moments in life that can change the course of our healing journey, and one such moment happened to me when I least expected it. Amid my recovery, I received a surprise visit from an old friend, the Black Priest, whom I had not anticipated seeing in the High Dependency Unit (HDU).

The visit that followed became a pivotal moment in my life, where I found the courage to share some of my deepest secrets and began to reclaim the power that had been taken from me. As we sat down and shared a bottle of coconut water, a treat his mother had sent me, I felt a sense of comfort and familiarity.

The Black Priest and his family had been a significant part of my life, and although we had been friends since childhood, there were still some things I had never shared with him. As we reminisced about a school camp we attended together, I divulged the dark memories that haunted me. I revealed to him that I had been drugged and that I believed I had been raped. It was a secret I had only shared with two other people and never with a man.

His response was compassionate and understanding as he looked into my eyes and offered a sincere apology for the pain I had endured. In that moment of vulnerability, I felt relief and empowerment. By sharing my story with someone who listened without judgement, I realised that I no longer needed to hold onto the secret that had caused me so much shame and humiliation. The weight of the burden began to lift, and I could start to regain some of the control that had been taken from me all those years ago.

I was not entirely certain of the truth of my experience; what mattered was that, at the time, it was real for me. By confiding in another person, I was able to reclaim my right to explore and define my own identity and sexuality, free from the constraints of fear and silence.

The Black Priest's visit became a turning point in my healing journey. It reminded me that sometimes the most powerful moments of growth come from sharing our deepest vulnerabilities with those who care for us. In doing so, we can break free from the chains that hold us back and move forward on the path to healing and self-discovery.

BLOG 7: Dialectics: A Path to Understanding and Resolving Conflicts

Generosity, and I found immense pleasure in discussing dialectics. It comforted us to know that we could reach an agreement by agreeing to disagree. Both sides of an argument can be right; we can both be right.

I read a passage from *DBT For Dummies* explaining how people often disagree. It is acceptable to disagree skilfully, see the wisdom from the other person's perspective, and let it be. This is known as 'agreeing to disagree'. Another possibility is that one or both parties acknowledge the other person's viewpoint as correct. This can occur when both individuals remain curious and open to the other's perspective or information. A third option involves developing a new perspective and synthesising each person's viewpoint. Throughout the process, you continually strive to open your mind to ideas or perspectives you may have missed.

To Generosity and me, dialectics seemed to solve all our problems. Generosity had encountered dialectics years ago during his philosophy studies, and it had resonated with him as a way to resolve conflicts. Whether we needed an answer during breakfast, lunch, or at other times, dialectics seemed to hold the key. It is all right to disagree because everyone's opinion is valid as it appears to them from their point of view. Each perspective is a person's best perspective at that moment. If it is right for them, it is all right for me. For Generosity and me, dialectics beautifully resolved every point of contention.

In a world where disagreements and conflicts seem ever-present, embracing dialectics to understand and resolve differences can lead to more harmonious relationships and deeper empathy. By acknowledging that multiple perspectives can hold truth, we can create a more open and accepting environment for communication and growth.

BLOG 8: Jacky's Spirit: A Journey Through the Richness of Aboriginal Culture

In my recent experiences, I connected with an Aboriginal Educator and Historian who generously shared his knowledge and passion for his culture. As a proud Gundungurra, Darug, and Kamilaroi person, he devoted his time to educating others about his people's rich history and traditions. This connection led us to embark on a journey of exploration, a project that would come to be known as 'Jacky's Spirit'.

Named in honour of the educator's grandmother, 'Jacky's Spirit' is a video project that captures the essence of Aboriginal culture through conversations with prominent elders and visits to historically significant locations. These sites include La Perouse (Lapa), Parramatta (George Street), St Marys, Yarramundi, and Katoomba, each bearing unique importance to Aboriginal people.

Our project also seeks to involve notable Aboriginal figures from various fields, such as sport and community leadership. By including these individuals, we aim to celebrate the accomplishments of the Aboriginal community while fostering a greater appreciation of their contributions to society.

As we embark on this journey, I have realised the power of acknowledging and honouring Aboriginal nations' connections to land, waters, and communities. By respecting the traditional custodians of these lands, we can contribute to a more unified and harmonious nation, embracing the wisdom and teachings passed down through generations.

'Jacky's Spirit' is more than a video project. It celebrates the rich tapestry of Aboriginal culture and explores the deep connections between people, land, and heritage. As we delve into the heart of Aboriginal history, we hope to share the beauty and strength of their spirit with the world, fostering greater understanding and appreciation for the traditions and values that have shaped their communities for thousands of years.

Andrew Turtle

Review: The Dialectics of Mania

The Dialectics of Mania offers a deeply introspective and thought-provoking exploration of mental health, particularly mania, through the lens of personal experience and broader systemic critique. The book is both a personal journey and a critique of the psychiatric system, with themes of self-advocacy, institutional limitations, and the often overlooked power of peer support. It provides a raw and honest narrative, illuminating the challenges of navigating mental health systems that often prioritise control over healing.

What stands out in the book is the duality between the internal experiences of mania, its highs, lows, and transformative potential, and the external forces of mental health care systems that can sometimes exacerbate the struggles of those affected. The author's experiences in a psychiatric ward highlight the stark contrast between the potential for compassionate care and the harsh realities of institutionalised treatment. This tension forms the core of the book's dialectic: the struggle between the individual's inner turmoil and the external system's response.

The theme of self-advocacy resonates deeply throughout the narrative. The author's reflections on their role as a consumer advocate and their disillusionment with the lack of progress in mental health care systems offer poignant commentary on the importance of systemic reform. The book emphasises that meaningful change in mental health care must involve improving access to services and recognising the value of peer support and patient-centred approaches to care.

Another key strength of the book is its exploration of the cyclical nature of mania and the transformative possibilities within the fluctuations of mental health. The author does not shy away from the complexities of their experiences, including moments of confusion, suffering, and frustration, but also finds moments of growth, understanding, and renewal. This theme highlights the healing potential even in the most difficult moments and invites readers to reflect on their own paths to understanding and managing their mental health.

One of the most powerful aspects of *The Dialectics of Mania* is its call for compassion and collaboration in mental health care. The author's critique of the psychiatric system is not merely a condemnation but a call to action for more empathetic, individualised care that respects patients' lived experiences. The book challenges the status quo by drawing attention to the absence of peer worker visits and the scarcity of meaningful interactions with staff. It offers a vision for a more supportive, collaborative approach to mental health care.

In conclusion, *The Dialectics of Mania* is a compelling and insightful work that blends personal narrative with critical analysis. It is an honest, vulnerable, and sometimes difficult read, but it provides valuable reflections on the intersections of mental health, advocacy, and systemic care. The author's journey is one of resilience, self-awareness, and a deep commitment to change, both within themselves and in the broader mental health landscape. The book is a powerful contribution to the ongoing conversation about mental health care and the need for more compassionate, transformative approaches to treatment.

The Dialectics of Mania holds significant potential in several key areas, offering valuable contributions to personal healing and the broader conversation about mental health care. Here are a few specific ways in which the book can have a powerful impact:

1. Catalyst for Reform in Mental Health Systems

The book's candid critique of the psychiatric system and the author's personal experiences make it a compelling piece for advocacy and systemic change. By shedding light on the flaws of institutionalised care, particularly the lack of meaningful support systems such as peer workers, the book has the potential to inspire discussions about how mental health care is structured. It could act as a call for reform, emphasising the need for greater empathy, more individualised care, and recognising peer support as an integral component of treatment.

2. Empowerment for Individuals with Lived Experience

For individuals living with mental health challenges, the book offers a sense of solidarity and empowerment. The author's openness about their experiences with mania, self-advocacy, and the ups and downs of their journey can resonate deeply with readers facing similar struggles. It may inspire others to be more vocal about their needs and advocate for themselves within the mental health system. The personal narrative also serves as a reminder that mental health challenges do not define one's identity; there is always room for growth, transformation, and renewal, even in the midst of turmoil.

3. Promoting Peer Support in Mental Health Care

The book makes a strong case for the value of peer workers in the mental health space, especially when dealing with trauma and complex needs. By drawing attention to the positive impact of peer support, or the lack thereof, *The Dialectics of Mania* could contribute to a shift in how mental health care is delivered, encouraging more institutions to integrate peer support systems into their models. Peer workers are uniquely positioned to connect with patients on a personal level, offering support that traditional medical staff may be unable to provide. The book amplifies the voices of those with lived experience, validating their expertise and encouraging mental health facilities to expand these roles.

4. A Resource for Mental Health Professionals

Mental health professionals, particularly those working in psychiatric settings, can benefit from reading *The Dialectics of Mania*. It provides a valuable perspective on how institutional practices impact the patients they serve and can help professionals better understand the importance of collaboration, compassion, and patient-centred care. The book serves as a reminder that the therapeutic relationship should be built on trust and partnership, not control and isolation.

5. A Guide for Personal Healing and Reflection

On a personal level, the book can be a valuable resource for individuals grappling with their mental health journeys, particularly those who experience manic episodes, psychosis, or similar challenges. The author's exploration of the highs and lows of mania and the eventual sense of renewal and purpose they find can offer hope and practical insight for those in similar circumstances. It presents the possibility of self-discovery, healing, and transformation, even in moments of great internal chaos.

6. Raising Awareness and Reducing Stigma

Through its honest portrayal of mania and mental health struggles, the book can help reduce stigma surrounding these conditions. It breaks down the often misunderstood nature of psychosis and mania, offering an empathetic and nuanced view that invites readers to consider the lived experience behind these diagnoses. As a result, it helps humanise mental health conditions, making them more understandable and relatable to a wider audience.

7. A Foundation for Further Research and Dialogue

The book can also spark academic and clinical discussions about the relationship between mental health and systemic issues, particularly around patient care and self-advocacy. Researchers, clinicians, and mental health policy experts may use insights from *The Dialectics of Mania* to further investigate the importance of peer support, the impact of institutionalised care on patients, and the benefits of a more human-centred approach to mental health treatment.

The potential of *The Dialectics of Mania* lies in its ability to inspire change on multiple levels, personal, professional, and institutional. It serves as a powerful tool for those navigating their mental health journeys while offering a critique of the systems meant to support them. By fostering deeper empathy, understanding, and advocacy for mental health reform, the book holds the potential to drive real and lasting change in how society views and treats mental health. Its intersection of personal experience and systemic critique places it at the forefront of contemporary discussions about mental health care.

Concluding Remarks

The Dialectics of Mania represents both a personal narrative and a profound exploration of mental health, systemic reform, and the complex nature of human experience. Through its vivid portrayal of struggles with mania and psychosis, alongside broader commentary on the mental health system, the book offers readers a unique perspective on the intersections between individual suffering and the need for systemic change. It reflects personal resilience and a call to improve mental health care, particularly within the lived experience movement.

The book has the potential to inspire others, both those living with mental health challenges and those working in the mental health field, to view mental health not as a static, singular condition but as a dynamic process deeply intertwined with systemic factors, cultural contexts, and personal histories. It highlights gaps in current care while offering hope for a future where empathy, collaboration, and innovation can lead to more compassionate, effective support systems.

From a technological perspective, the ideas presented in the book could lead to advancements in digital therapeutics, peer support, and patient-centred care. By harnessing technology and human connection, the book can drive positive change in mental health advocacy, care practices, and research.

Ultimately, *The Dialectics of Mania* challenges the reader to confront uncomfortable truths about mental health care while offering a pathway to healing and understanding. It is a testament to the power of lived experience and a reminder that progress often comes from the courage to speak out, the willingness to listen, and the collective effort to create lasting change.

www.ingramcontent.com/pod-product-compliance
Lightning Source LLC
LaVergne TN
LVHW022219200926
848481LV00006B/2027
* 9 7 8 1 9 1 8 9 0 0 0 0 2 *